Bonding

MARSHALL H. KLAUS, M.D.,
is Adjunct Professor of Pediatrics at the University of California, San Francisco. A distinguished neonatologist and researcher, he is the author or co-author of several standard works in the field, including *Maternal–Infant Bonding, Parent–Infant Bonding, Care of the High-Risk Infant, The Amazing Newborn, Mothering the Mother,* and an editor of the *Yearbook of Neonatal and Perinatal Medicine.*

JOHN H. KENNELL, M.D., is Professor of Pediatrics at Case Western Reserve University School of Medicine and Chief of the Division of Child Development at Rainbow Babies and Children's Hospital in Cleveland, Ohio. In addition to his ongoing research on the doula and on perinatal influences on parents and infants, his teaching and patient care, he continues to participate each year with medical students who serve as apprentice-physician doulas for mothers. He is the co-author of *Maternal–Infant Bonding, Parent–Infant Bonding,* and *Mothering the Mother.*

PHYLLIS H. KLAUS, C.S.W., M.F.C.C., formerly on the faculty of the Department of Family Practice, Michigan State University, now teaches and practices at the Erickson Institute in Santa Rosa and also practices in Berkeley, California, providing psychotherapy and especially working with the concerns, both medical and psychological, of pregnancy, birth, and the postpartum period. She consults nationally and internationally, does research, and is co-author of *The Amazing Newborn* and *Mothering the Mother.*

Bonding

BUILDING THE FOUNDATIONS
OF SECURE ATTACHMENT
AND INDEPENDENCE

Marshall H. Klaus, M.D.

John H. Kennell, M.D.

Phyllis H. Klaus, C.S.W., M.F.C.C.

A Mandarin Paperback
BONDING

First published in the United States of America
by Addison-Wesley Publishing Company Inc.
First published in Great Britain 1996
as a Cedar Original
by Mandarin Paperbacks
an imprint of Reed International Books Ltd
Michelin House, 81 Fulham Road, London SW3 6RB
and Auckland, Melbourne, Singapore and Toronto

Portions of Chapters 2, 4, 7 and 8 are adapted from
Parent–Infant Bonding, 2nd ed. St. Louis, MO:
C.V. Mosby, 1982.

A CIP catalogue record for this title
is available from the British Library
ISBN 0 7493 2254 3

Printed and bound in Great Britain
by Cox & Wyman Ltd, Reading, Berks

Contents

We dedicate this book to all the mothers and fathers—and their infants—who, by their actions and words, have opened our eyes to the wonders and powerful events occurring in the early hours, days, and weeks of life.

We anticipate that what they have shown us—and what we have reported in this book—will lead to more humanistic care-giving practices for the mother and father during labor and for the family in the early postpartum period.

Acknowledgments

We are indebted to the many medical students, nurses, research assistants, and colleagues who have contributed their thoughts and energy so generously. We appreciate the wise counsel and research information provided by numerous investigators and clinicians in nursing, pediatrics, obstetrics, developmental psychology, psychiatry, psychoanalysis, social work, animal behavior, and anthropology. Our special thanks to our editor, Merloyd Lawrence, for her patience, encouragement, sensitive understanding of this field, and unique editing skills.

Generous financial support and encouragement provided by the William T. Grant Foundation, the Thrasher Foundation, Irving Harris and the Pittway Foundation, the Research Corporation, the Arthur Vining Davis Foundation, the Educational Foundation of America, Maternal and Child Health Bureau, and for the last thirteen years, NICHD Grant #HD16915 have made our research and this book possible.

Foreword

BY T. BERRY BRAZELTON, M.D.

Parents are fortunate indeed to have this firsthand elaboration of the "bonding process" from such distinguished clinicians and researchers as Drs. Klaus and Kennell, together with Phyllis Klaus. I can remember when Marshall Klaus and John Kennell conceived of their now-classic research to change delivery practices all over the United States. At that time, the delivery of a normal, healthy infant to a normal, healthy woman was treated as a pathological medical event and conducted as if it were a surgical procedure subject to dangerous consequences.

In the process of devising sterile, safe delivery techniques for mothers and of developing the technology and practices for safe and effective caring for newborns, we created an aura of pathology and medical control around the entire delivery process. As we grew more comfortable about the issues of safety and sterility, it became apparent that we had ignored the personal issues of the parents involved. They were feeling like passive patients rather than new parents wanting (and needing) to feel competent and in control as they began parenting their new infant. The premedication that made labor and delivery relatively painless and controllable by medical personnel was found to leave mothers and their infants depressed and relatively unresponsive, even days after delivery. In addition, medicated laboring mothers felt "out of control" and at the mercy of others, when they wanted to feel effective and autonomous. Fathers, long excluded from the whole process, felt left out and useless, when they should have been included and supported.

In the 1950s reports had begun to reach the United States from Europe that there was a "new" way for women to be awake and participating in the delivery process. Women seemed able to survive and even master the pain of delivery—and felt proud of that! Childbirth Education Association groups began to spring up all over the United States. Supportive groups of nurses, physicians, and parents who had gone through the process began to form, and parents-to-be found that education before labor and a minimum of support during labor made a nonmedicated, participant labor an effective and exciting way of delivering babies.

As a pediatrician interested in newborns' responsive behavior and their ability to capture parents with their alertness in the early neonatal period, I was a strong supporter of returning to more "natural" childbirth practices that included active participation of both parents. As we looked at the newborns of nonmedicated, awake mothers, we found that the babies were significantly more responsive at delivery. In the delivery room these babies would turn toward voices and search for faces. When they saw someone's face, their own faces would brighten, as if to say, "There you are! You're talking to me, and I want to know you!" If we gave such a newborn a choice between my male voice and the mother's, the baby would inevitably turn to the mother's, search for her face, and find it. At this point every mother would automatically reach for the baby to cuddle and would realize or say,

"You know me already." This situation is typical of many in which newborns naturally begin to capture and excite new parents. When newborns are alert for their parents and responsive to their parents' efforts to communicate, the parents' feelings are enhanced in the process that Klaus and Kennell have labeled as "bonding." This book brings into focus the many valuable ways both professionals and parents can participate to enhance these opportunities.

During these years when childbirth practices were changing, I was involved in research with psychoanalysts at the Putnam Children's Center in Boston, where we studied the processes by which parents adjust to their new responsibilities. In the last half of the pregnancy both parents went through a predictable kind of turmoil—"Will I ever get to be a parent? Will I make it as a parent, or will I ruin my baby? If I get to be a parent, will I have to be like my parent? I certainly don't want to be like that!" Realizing that their only past experience with parenthood was their own upbringing made them wary of the process and afraid of failure in the task that lay ahead. As they questioned themselves, they began to wonder: "Have we made a mistake? Do we really want this baby?" And if they weren't sure that they wanted the infant, they asked themselves, "Could we have already damaged the baby by being ambivalent?" We also found that all parents-to-be rehearsed for a damaged infant, and new parents felt it was their fault if the baby was impaired in any way.

As we uncovered this turmoil in pregnancy, we began to wonder why it was so universal and why it dominated the emotions during the last part of pregnancy. Such universals always seem to be adaptive, and I began to realize that the purpose and the goal for this turmoil was for the adults to mobilize all their available emotional energy in making the tremendous adjustment to parenthood and bonding with their special baby. In other words, their self-questioning was really covering a kind of "alarm" reaction that mobilized their energy to search for and find the special capacities of their new infant and to parent that baby successfully. I see this as an adaptive process, one that helps a person become "ready" to parent at or soon after delivery. The authors of this book recognize this energy and show that it is available at delivery for parents to bond to their new infant.

It is in this area of bonding to the new infant that Marshall Klaus and John Kennell's work has made such a universal, powerful impact. Their research and follow-up with parents who remain alert during delivery and available in the delivery room to hold, to nestle, and to nurse the newborn have changed hospital and delivery practices all over the world. Most hospital staffs are aware of the implications of their work, and most all have now begun to change in the direction of parental participation in the mode and conduct of delivery. We are seeing the fruits of this. Parents feel stronger, more in control of the delivery, and more confident of their abilities as new parents. Studies of their children at one, two, three, and seven years of age have indicated that they show improved performance in several areas. My own interpretation is that the improved self-images of the parents are handed on directly to the infants and are likely to be manifested later in the form of improved performances—in tests, in school, and in general.

Since this research has achieved recognition, it has become apparent to all of us in the work of supporting parents that initial bonding is not enough. Bonding may be like falling in love, but there are years ahead when it is likely to be increasingly difficult to stay in love. The work of being a parent becomes harder and more critical as time goes on. This book gives the necessary support to parents who are working toward strengthening the bond through the vicissitudes of parenthood. The thrill of starting off successfully certainly can enhance one's expectation about being a parent. But it is not the only source of energy for attachment. The infant's development is a source of constant excitement, and it is both amazing and rewarding for parents to follow and participate in each developmental step of their newborn. In this way babies become powerful participants in their own development, and the initial energy put into the bonding process can be translated into developing lasting attachments.

Backed up by such books as this, and by professionals familiar with this research, parents will feel more and more competent in their roles and will pass on this feeling to their newborns and older children. A sense of parental competence is at the base of improved performance, especially in the ability to give to others and to parent and bond with future children more successfully.

Thanks to the continuing work of John Kennell and Marshall and Phyllis Klaus, we know the behavioral sequences in the bonding process between new parents and infants. Their more recent work on the effect of doulas (women who offer continuous personal support to mothers in labor) shows how critical it is to have such trained support during labor and delivery. Despite criticism by some that "proof" of a sensitive period for bonding between parent and baby has not been shown, the authors have continued to fight for a more humane atmosphere in hospitals at the time of delivery. This humanized atmosphere includes time for early attachment behavior between a new parent and baby. We now recognize how critical it is to create this atmosphere of respect and support, and to capture the passionate feelings that are optimized at the end of labor and delivery.

With today's relentless "progress" toward shortened stays in maternity hospitals, all of the recommendations of these three dedicated clinicians and researchers are becoming increasingly important. We had better listen to them.

T. Berry Brazelton, M.D.
Professor Emeritus, Pediatrics
Harvard Medical School
Founder, Child Development Unit
Children's Hospital, Boston

Introduction

Parents want the world for their children. They want their children to be healthy, happy, and independent, to be curious about life, to be loving and responsive, to develop healthy relationships, to feel secure and good about themselves, and to weather difficult life situations. When uninterrupted by unforeseen or unrecognized obstacles, parents will go to great lengths to provide these advantages for their children. Such powerful motivation also enables parents to see their children for their own sakes and not to project onto them their own unresolved anxieties or traumas. They find within themselves the ability to respond beyond the call of simple duty to their child's needs and feelings. When parents are able to provide such an environment for their children, it is more likely that the children, in turn, will develop a sense of secure attachment to them and a subsequent healthy sense of self in the world.

In our lifetime there has been an expansion of understanding of how parents develop these life enhancing nurturant qualities and of how these shape a child's development. We believe that part of this development is a process by which parents form bonds to their children. This process is not an isolated occurrence but takes place on a continuum of experience, from their own upbringing to the events around pregnancy, birth, the postpartum period, and the beginning months of life. We also believe that certain settings and certain kinds of support can help parents form these bonds and nurture their children successfully. We believe that creating a calm, emotionally supportive, and responsive environment during labor, birth, and the early postpartum period can offer a model of caring, which for some parents may actually provide a type of reparenting. For all parents, such caring brings an internalized sense of being nurtured, secure, and validated, an experience that they, in turn, are more able to provide for their child.

The parents' bond to their child may be not only the strongest but also the most important of human attachments. Though newborns are active and aware, they cannot manage on their own, and the bonds from the caretaker, usually the mother and father, to the infant are crucial for the baby's survival and development. The power of this attachment is so great that it enables the mother and father to make the continuous sacrifices necessary for the care of an infant—attending to crying, protecting the baby from danger, and giving feedings in the middle of the night, despite their own desperate need to sleep.

By general consensus, the term *bonding* refers to the tie from parent to infant, whereas the word *attachment* refers to the tie from infant to parent. In this book we will sometimes also use the word *attachment* in its more generally understood meaning, referring to the feelings that bind one person to another, in either direction. While parent–infant bonding, as we shall see, has certain recurring characteristics, it is not fixed or uniform. The setting, the circumstances, the family's history, and individual differences affect its course. Some misinterpreta-tion of studies in this area may have resulted from a too-literal interpretation of the word *bonding* as meaning an event as instantaneous and predictable as the application of epoxy.

A *bond* can be defined as a unique relationship between two people that is specific and endures through time. Although it is difficult to define this enduring relationship operationally, we have taken as indicators of this attachment various kinds of behavior between parents and infants, such as kissing, cuddling, and prolonged gazing—behavior that maintains contact and exhibits one's affection toward a particular individual. While indicators are useful in experimental observations, it is important to distinguish between a bond and bonding or between attachment and attachment behavior. Parental bonds can persist during long separations of time and distance, even though visible signs of their existence often may not be apparent. A call for help even after forty years will bring a mother to her child and evoke signs of affection and closeness equal in strength to those in the first year of life.

Much of the joy and sorrow in our lives revolves around attachments—making them, breaking them, preparing for them, and adjusting to their loss through death. Each of us may have hundreds of acquaintances in a lifetime, but at any one time we are closely attached to only a small number of people. Much of the richness and beauty of life derives from these close relationships, these attachments to mother, father, brother, sister, husband, wife, son, daughter, and a small cadre of close friends. This book deals with one of these special relationships—the bond a mother or father forms with his or her newborn infant, and its effect on the attachment from infant to parent.

Major workers in the field have variously described attachment in the parent–infant relationship. The psychoanalysts James and Joyce Robertson[1] spoke of a parental phenomenon characterized by a "one-way flow of concern and affection" for children nurtured through infancy. They saw a direct relationship between the degree of parental involvement initially and the intensity of the bond, which is generally stronger in the mother, somewhat less strong in the father, and gradually less strong among other family members. In trying to convey the force of this feeling, the great British pediatrician and psychoanalyst D. W. Winnicott[2] described a mother's love as a pretty crude affair: "There's a possessiveness in it, there's appetite in it, there is a 'Drat the kid' element in it, there's generosity in it, there's power in it, as well as humility, but sentimentality is outside of it altogether and is repugnant to mothers." The psychiatrist John Bowlby,[3] describing bonds of affection in more general terms, wrote:

> Affectional bonds and subjective states of a strong emotion tend to go together as every novelist and playwright knows. Thus many of the most intensive of all emotions arise during the formation, the maintenance, the disruption and renewal of affectional bonds which for that reason are sometimes called emotional bonds. In terms of subjective experience the formation of a bond is described as falling in love, maintaining a bond as loving someone, and losing a partner as grieving over someone. Similarly the threat of a loss arouses anxiety and actual loss causes sorrow, while both situations are likely to arouse anger. Finally the unchallenged maintenance of a bond is experienced as a source of security and a renewal of a bond as a source of joy.

As authors and investigators trying to understand attachment and bonding, we are fortunate that these topics have been studied intensively during the past half century by talented and creative observers. Among the landmark works are those of the psychoanalyst René Spitz, who showed the importance of parental bonding by describing the results of its absence.[4] He observed that infants in foundling homes with adequate food but without loving attention and caretaking did not grow or develop and often died. Bowlby and Winnicott documented how the parents' own mothering became an inner working model for their own future caretaking, and the psychoanalyst Selma Fraiberg observed how ghosts of past experiences in early life could deeply affect parental feelings and behavior.[5] The psychologist Mary Ainsworth identified how necessary it is for an infant to have a sensitive and responsive mother in order to develop a secure base for future development, and she also observed that a child's style of attachment and separation behavior is related to his or her early parenting.[6]

During the late 1950s and 1960s the detailed studies of maternal and infant behavior in animals by such investigators as Harry Harlow, Harriet Rheingold, Jay Rosenblatt, T. C. Schneirla, Patrick Bateson, and others were both a stimulus and special help in the design of studies exploring human maternal behavior. At about the same time, the analyst Greta Bibring and psychoanalytically-trained pediatrician T. Berry Brazelton uncovered anxiety and distorted unconscious material among normal pregnant women. Brazelton noted how this turmoil "mobilizes the positive forces for caring."[7] The infant research of Brazelton, Daniel Stern, Colwyn Trevarthan, and Louis Sander explored and began to decode the intimate beginning interactions between mothers and their infants. It is against this impressive background that our interest in exploring parent–infant bonds, and the settings and care that enhance them, began to unfold in the early 1970s.

To understand the situation in which our research began, one must be familiar with the way maternity hospitals and newborn nurseries were run at the time. Concern about protecting patients from the very real danger of contagious disorders led to sometimes extreme policies of isolation and separation. Fear about the spread of infection accounted for the physical separation of the obstetrical and pediatric divisions in large general hospitals. Not only was diarrhea epidemic, but respiratory infections were a scourge of children's hospitals and maternity and infant units. As a result of infection problems, maternity hospitals gathered full-term babies in large nurseries in a fortresslike arrangement. Germs were the enemy; therefore, parents and families who might have carried them were excluded.

The rigid rules in the newborn nursery were maintained until the early 1970s when family-centered care on the delivery floor began, and parents were invited into the premature nursery. Then, the gates of the obstetric floor were opened, and the father and other close family members were permitted to visit with the newborn in the mother's room for an extended time. Gradually in the 1980s mothers were encouraged to have their infants with them for prolonged periods, both to improve the success of lactation and to enable them to become better acquainted. With the very short hospital stays of twenty-four to forty-eight hours instituted in the 1990s, new obstetrical units are now being built with mother and baby sharing a room, and newborn nurseries for normal infants are being made much smaller to care for only the infants of mothers who are ill and the few newborns who require observation.

Since the early 1970s, other important transitions in medical care have occurred. The crucial life events surrounding the development of both attachment and detachment (through death) have been removed from the home and brought into the hospital. The hospital now determines the procedures involved in both birth and death. The experiences surrounding these two events in the life of an individual have been stripped of the long-established traditions and support systems built up over centuries to help families through these highly meaningful transitions.

Over many years, two of the authors of this book, John H. Kennell and Marshall H. Klaus, have had the opportunity to observe how new parents adapt. In our pediatric work with normal, healthy, full-term infants and their mothers, and with sick infants in the intensive care nursery and the mothers and fathers who are separated from them, we have been led to ask the question, "What is the process by which a father and mother become attached to an infant?" This is our continuing quest, and in this book we describe what we have learned. We have developed ever-greater respect for the complexities of the process by which this occurs. At the same time, we have felt a new excitement about the opportunities parents have for major psychological growth with the birth of an infant and about the orchestration of the many biological systems that are integrated into the attachment sequence.

Phyllis H. Klaus, the third author, has had extensive clinical experience as a psychotherapist caring for families as they adjust to a new baby and for women with medical and psychological problems during pregnancy and the perinatal period. She helps adults, including expectant parents, find ways to repair the traumas they may have suffered as children. Questions of bonding and attachment have become equally compelling in her work.

What triggers, fosters, or disturbs a parent's bond to his or her infant? In an attempt to answer this question, we have gathered information from a wide range of sources, including (1) clinical observations during medical-care procedures; (2) naturalistic observations of parenting; (3) long-term, in-depth interviews of a small number of mothers, primarily by psychologists and psychoanalysts; (4) structured interviews or observations; and (5) results from closely controlled studies on the parents of both premature and full-term infants.

All of these observations and studies must be considered within the framework of the social setting. Cultural influences, the values and expectations of both the mother and the observer, and hospital structures and policies all influence the final outcome. Even in our modern health-care system, behaviors and practices surrounding birth vary widely. Practices that seem to work well for one group are not necessarily optimal solutions for those in another culture, and what seems to be "natural" is not necessarily "good" for all.

With this caveat in mind, we begin piecing together components of the affectional bond between a mother, a father, and an infant and determining the factors that may alter or distort its formation. Since newborns are wholly dependent on their mothers or fathers to meet all their physical and emotional needs, the strength and durability of the parental bonds may well determine whether or not the babies will develop optimally.

Events that are important to the formation of the parent–infant bond include:

Planning the pregnancy
Confirming the pregnancy
Accepting the pregnancy
Becoming aware of fetal movement (quickening)
Perceiving the fetus as a separate individual
Experiencing labor
Giving birth
Seeing the baby
Touching the baby
Caring for the baby
Accepting the infant as a separate individual into the family

By observing and studying the mother and father during each of these periods, we can begin to fit together the inter-locking pieces that lay the foundations of the parent–infant relationship.

From our fumbling, early efforts to understand and unravel the mysteries of the bonding process, we have developed our present understanding, which evolves continually. Although our early behavioral observations often stimulated productive studies, they often misled us in our understanding of a specific phenomenon. For example, when we first permitted mothers to enter the premature nursery to touch their infants in the incubator, we noticed that they would poke at their infants as women poke a cake to test whether it is done, touching the tips of their fingers to their infants' extremities. We wondered about the origins of this behavior. Our thoughts and ideas about it have evolved as we have gone back and forth from the intensive care unit to the normal full-term nursery. As noted in Chapter 7, poking at premature infants by mothers is possibly a variation of the normal maternal behavior in response to an infant who appears fragile and to an incubator that is standing in the way. When the full-term infant and mother are in a situation more appropriate for their becoming acquainted, this behavior is observed only during the first minutes of contact.

In Chapter 1, "Pregnancy: New Connections Begin," we explore how pregnancy alters the attachment process and what effects the new reproductive technologies such as ultrasound and amniocentesis may have on the future relationship. Special precon-ceptual care designed to reduce the incidence of congenital mal-formation is also examined from this point of view. In Chapter 2, "Labor and Birth," we explore the dual effect on the parent–infant relationship of the emotional and physical care of the mother dur-ing labor. Not only can this significantly decrease many complica-tions of labor including cesarean sections and thus change the first encounter between parent and infant, but it can also directly affect a woman's feelings about her infant and her partner.

Since attachment is not a one-way street, we examine in Chapter 3, "What the Baby Brings," the many resources and talents a newborn has available when first meeting the mother and father. Learning about these will help parents find the amazing capacities and unique characteristics of their baby and discover more quickly how to meet their infant's needs.

In Chapter 4, "Birth of a Family: The First Minutes and Hours," we describe the many physical and emotional events in the infant and mother that are set in motion at birth, including hor-monal and immunologic systems; the senses of smell, touch, and sight; and the first gestures toward one another. We also explore how the newly discovered ability of infants to crawl to the mother's breast and latch onto the nipple unaided can be incorporated into care that maximizes the early connections for mother and baby. We look at the effect and, in our view, importance of a time alone for the new family in the first hour of life, and we describe the many research studies that relate to these topics.

Since in the early days and weeks of life feeding plays such a central role in a mother and infant's time together, we examine in Chapter 5, "Infant Feeding and the Beginning of Intimacy," simple maneuvers that help make feeding enjoyable and successful and that enhance the mother–infant relationship. In Chapter 6, "Developing Ties: The First Days and Weeks," we look closely at the reasons why additional support systems for the mother and father are so vital in decreasing postpartum depression and in helping the adjustment to a new family. When all goes well during this time, a gradual strengthening of ties between parent and infant occurs.

In Chapter 7, "Premature Birth and Bonding," we look at the parent–infant relationship in the very different circumstances of prematurity. We describe new care procedures that help parents adapt to their premature infants, including nesting, kangaroo care, and living-in with the infant. An understanding of how small premature infants develop compared with babies born at term can also help this relationship. In Chapter 8, "Birth Defects and Bonding," we explore how parents manage after the birth of a malformed infant and what can help or harm their adaptation.

In Chapter 9, "Bonding: The Route to Independence," we give our views on the way a strong parent–infant bond— enhanced by continuous emotional support during labor, birth, and the postpartum period—improves parents' responsiveness to their baby's multiple needs and, in turn, strengthens the attachment the infant makes with his or her parents. We also describe parents and their children who have had early difficulties in this relationship, and we show how some problems in parental attachment can be corrected and resolved over a relatively short time.

1

PREGNANCY:
NEW CONNECTIONS BEGIN

When a woman and her partner first hear the news of their pregnancy, they feel a rush of emotions. Some couples are ecstatic, while others have mixed reactions.

However, after the initial excitement, everyone—even the most enthusiastic couple—will have all sorts of questions. How will I handle my job? Where will we put the baby? Will I be able to graduate? Can we afford it? Are we really ready? Are we prepared to give up our present life? How does my partner truly feel about the baby? Some women who have previously had problems with a pregnancy ask themselves more questions: Since it was so hard to become pregnant, will I be able to carry the baby? Will the baby be normal? Should we wait for the screening tests and amniocentesis results before we tell our families?

For everyone, pregnancy is a major developmental milestone and, whether this is a first or subsequent pregnancy, it is a significant life event and stirs up many memories or experiences, either remembered or forgotten. In every family the relationship with the baby-to-be grows in a different physical and emotional environment.

BEFORE PREGNANCY

Among the many positive influences on a couple's reaction to a pregnancy is their general feeling of readiness to nurture a child. Have they had the chance to be together and know each other well enough to make this decision? Are they supportive of each other in the decision to have a baby, whether it is their first baby or their third? One partner often takes more time before being ready for a second. A pregnancy undertaken at a time of serious illness or death of a family member will bear added stress. Do both parents feel ready financially to take on a new baby? If at all possible, a couple should discuss previous issues surrounding childbirth and previous pregnancies, such as abortions, stillbirths, miscarriages, or traumatic birth experiences, with a doctor and, when appropriate, a psychological caregiver. Many health concerns can be alleviated with advance planning. For instance, women with diabetes should know that with tight control of their blood sugar before conception, the risk of congenital malformations is not greater than for other mothers.[1] As another example, all women planning a pregnancy should begin to take 0.8 milligrams of folic acid a day, starting three to four weeks before conception. This has been shown to reduce significantly the incidence of certain malformations in infants.[2]

Women with physical disabilities and women without support at home do well to work out arrangements in advance for help in managing their own care and that of the new baby after the birth. If they can do so before conception, the period of pregnancy will be much less stressful. Women who wish to stop smoking, drinking, or engaging in other drug abuse need to get help in reducing these practices before they become pregnant. In this way, a mother can avoid adding complex layers of guilt to the emerging relationship. Fortunately, proven techniques can help people recover from these habits. If a future parent experienced childhood sexual abuse, it is essential before starting a pregnancy to address this issue with specialized help and to work out concerns that individual might have.

LEARNING TO CARE

A mother and father's past experiences are a major determinant in molding their caregiving role. Children use adults, especially loved and powerful adults, as models for their own behavior. "Playing house," an activity that dominates the waking hours of children, especially girls, during the preschool years, appears to be a preparatory rehearsal for nurturing a real baby two or three decades later. Parents who watch their preschoolers are continually surprised to find that their children imitate their own actions, attitudes, and facial movements in the most minute detail. A striking, if unusual, illustration of how early caretaking of an infant, taken in by the child through a complex mental process, becomes a template for her own parenting in later life is found in the following case. Monica was born with a section of her esophagus completely closed.[3] She required tube feedings into her stomach and was never held in anyone's arms for feeding. At twenty-one months, surgery established the passage between Monica's mouth and stomach. Films made over the next thirty years of her life showed that in every feeding situation she repeated her own early feeding experience. She never held her doll in her arms as a little girl. Later, when she was responsible for babies as an adolescent babysitter or when she cared for her own four infants, she never held them in her arms. The doll was placed on a couch to be fed, and Monica put each of her four babies facing her on her knees as she sat. Monica also played with her babies in the same way she had been played with, that is, only when they were flat on their backs for diapering or a bath. Despite other examples around her and recommendations, Monica held her dolls and children as she had been held as an infant. Her own experience in infancy became an enduring model for her caretaking as a baby-sitter and a mother. This pattern even began to carry into another generation. Her own four daughters held their dolls in a like manner when they first began to play with them. Interestingly, these little girls as infants had been fed once a day in their father's arms. By the age of five, each of these daughters had moved the dolls into her arms in the closely held traditional position.

Thus, long before a woman herself becomes a mother, she has learned from the way she was mothered and through observation, play, and practice a repertoire of mothering behaviors. She has already learned whether or not infants are picked up when they cry, how much they are carried, and whether they should be chubby or thin. These "facts," taken in when children are very young, become unquestioned imperatives throughout life. Unless adults consciously and painstakingly reexamine these learned attitudes and behaviors, they will unconsciously repeat them when they become parents.

Children and adolescents need experiences nurturing and providing care for smaller children and babies to prepare them for parenthood. Many young women and men have had no exposure to caretaking of children before they have their own. If they have never handled an infant or cared for a small child, new mothers and fathers are inexperienced and relatively helpless when they begin to care for their own newborn infant. In our work, we have often recommended that expectant parents arrange to care for the young infant of one of their friends on two or three occasions; for example, for half a day and then building up to a full day and perhaps an overnight stay. The experience will prove invaluable when they face the challenge of handling their own infant, and their friends will be most grateful for the time together away from the responsibility of caring for their baby.

These planned experiences replace the traditional experiences of most young girls in developing countries. In large families girls are often expected to assume the care of young infants until they deliver their own. Such experience allows young women to make fine adjustments in their mothering styles and to gain a wealth of confidence before becoming mothers themselves. In all cultures, the way parents are raised, which includes both the practices of the culture and the idiosyncrasies of their parents' child-rearing practices, greatly influences their behavior toward their own infant.

Many people believe that since the bonding of parents to their small infant occurs naturally, it could be a mistake to make too much of it. This may be true in general, but a number of women (and men) have a difficult time making this adjustment and becoming bonded.[4] Although pregnancy is a perfectly normal event, it also represents a "dangerous opportunity" because, as with any momentous change, it is a turning point in an individual's life, particularly if it is a first pregnancy. The outcome of the crisis will powerfully affect the developing parent–child relationship. By understanding the beginning of the parent–infant bond, we may be better able to provide help and a supportive setting as needed by new parents.

REACTIONS TO PREGNANCY

During pregnancy a woman concurrently experiences two types of developmental changes: (1) her own physical and emotional changes and (2) the growth of the fetus in her uterus. The way she feels about these changes will vary widely, according to whether she planned the pregnancy, has a partner, is living with the father, has support in her home, or has other children. Her feelings will also be influenced by the ages of her other children, her occupation or her desire for one, her memories of her own childhood, and her feelings about her parents. For most women, pregnancy is a time of strong and changing emotions, ranging from positive to negative and, frequently, ambivalent. With the realization that she will soon have a baby, particularly if it is her first, the woman must begin to adapt to a dramatic shift in her lifestyle, as she changes from an individual responsible primarily for herself to a parent responsible for a child's life and well-being. Fathers also feel great emotional changes as their priorities change and added financial requirements loom ahead.

Some women sense a change from the moment of conception and know they are pregnant before they miss a period. Others develop the feeling of bearing a child more gradually. Seeing some movement of the baby on ultrasound imaging early in pregnancy and feeling the sensation of fetal movement, often called "quickening", around five months are two other ways that women begin to develop a connection to the baby within. At this point, a woman will usually begin to have fantasies about what the baby will be like, imagining particular personality characteristics and developing early feelings of bonding. As a result, she may further accept her pregnancy. Unplanned, unwanted infants may begin to seem more acceptable at this point. Parents may now feel ready to make preparations; they may purchase clothes or a crib, select a name, and rearrange their home to accommodate a baby.

In one Australian study, researchers explored the feelings and thoughts of thirty mothers during their first pregnancies.[5] In the first interview at eight to twelve weeks, 70 percent of these women said they could not believe that the fetus was really there, and they never imagined or pictured it. To them the fetus was not a real person. The others believed that the fetus was a real person, and they spontaneously imagined its appearance. These women were likely to describe the fetus with a feeling of concern. They predicted severe grief if they were to have a miscarriage. Feelings of bonding were inhibited when severe physical problems of pregnancy existed or when the woman's husband was not interested in the fetus or did not provide her with emotional support. After the interview, mothers were asked to draw an image of the fetus. During the eight- to twelve-week gestation period, the fetus was presented as shapeless and formless, but as the pregnancy progressed, the fetus developed a more human form.

T. Berry Brazelton has clarified the importance of the changes and turmoil that occur during pregnancy for the subsequent development of attachment to the new infant.[6] Noting the anxiety characteristic of a mother pregnant with her first child, he has addressed this initial concern about being able to adjust to mothering. What happens, he believes, is that in some way this anxiety, instead of being a destructive force, "mobilizes the energy" necessary to the huge job ahead. He sees the "shakeup of pregnancy as readying the circuits for new attachments, as preparation for the many choices which 'a mother' must be ready to make . . . [and] as a method of freeing her circuits for a kind of sensitivity to the infant and his individual requirements."[7] He notes that this is an example of how physicians might label a mother as "anxious" or as "needing help" when her responses are more accurately described as normal anxiety. He believes that reassuring a mother that her feelings are a normal, healthy sign of caring is an essential step in establishing her confidence and preparedness as a new parent.

HELP FOR ANXIETY AND STRESS

Although Brazelton and others recognize this normal process of adjusting to the pregnancy as a cause of much anxiety, some women who appear anxious or describe their anxiety to a caregiver may require additional help to resolve these feelings. Anxiousness and a sense of stress can affect how a woman feels about herself and the baby and can release stress hormones. These may affect the pregnancy by creating symptoms that are frightening or that make a woman feel less in control.

To alleviate anxiety and help women recognize when they are stressed, one must listen closely to women to hear their concerns and their thoughts. Often, just listening reduces these anxieties, and the anxieties can be reframed as normal responses to being pregnant. However, current stressors in the woman's life may be precipitating the anxiety and may need to be addressed. At the same time, pregnancy is a period of unusual openness in both parents. The woman needs to be "physiologically open" to take on the fetus and "psychologically open" to take in the infant-to-be. Fathers also experience a psychological openness that may trigger confusing feelings for them. This openness may allow unconscious and unresolved issues of the past to be stirred up and bubble to the surface, creating overwhelming feelings of anxiety and sometimes symptoms that require exploration and resolution.

Any stress—such as a move to a new geographic area, marital infidelity, the death of a close friend or relative, earlier abortions, or the loss of previous children—that leaves the mother feeling unloved or unsupported or that precipitates concern for the health and survival of either her infant or herself may delay preparation for the infant and retard bond formation. After the first trimester, behaviors that are a reaction to stress and suggest a rejection of pregnancy include a preoccupation with physical appearance or a negative self-perception, excessive emotional withdrawal or mood swings, unusual anxiety or feelings of depression, excessive physical complaints, absence of any response to quickening, or the lack of any preparatory behavior during the last trimester.

Asking a woman how she is feeling, how she is doing, what concerns or fears she has, and what problems she is facing can help her begin to release internalized fears and feelings just by allowing her to talk about them. A sensitive, empathic listener can validate a woman's feelings and let her know that somebody hears and understands. At other times a helpful listener can help the woman clarify her concerns and begin to work on resolving them. If the anxiety does not diminish, more emotional probing may need to take place with someone skilled in this area.

The last several decades have brought more understanding of how the mind affects the body; whole new fields, such as psycho-neuroimmunology, have been developed to study these effects. Studies have shown that if individuals are depressed, their immuno-logical defenses are markedly weakened, and they are much more susceptible to infection. Just as fear or stress can raise the heart rate or make muscles tighten, similar emotions, conscious or uncon-scious, can affect the physical systems involved in pregnancy and labor. Some of the medical complications of pregnancy, including *hyperemesis gravidarum* (continual vomiting requiring admission to a hospital so one can get intravenous fluids), premature labor, bleed-ing, intrauterine failure to grow, and other conditions,[8] have been successfully treated with psychotherapy and techniques such as hypnosis. The following brief cases from our experience offer a glimpse of the power of unresolved emotional experience and the possibility of changing the course of a difficult pregnancy.

Debra was referred by her obstetrician because at five months gestation she had "no feelings for the baby," and the baby was not growing. In discussing her feelings, she expressed anger and discouragement with her husband. She had been the main financial support in the family for the past five years, and now that she was pregnant, she felt hurt because he did not take more inter-est or feel responsible for taking care of her. However, she did not feel comfortable in talking to him about this or expressing both her sadness and her anger. At the same time, she was not properly caring for herself. In trying to understand how all this had come about, she began to recall certain important events in her life. Debra remembered as a very young child being severely repri-manded by her father. She had felt humiliated and frightened, and had developed a belief that she could never talk back to a man—

that was too frightening. Because of this fear, Debra protected herself and did not act naturally with her father or, in later life, with any other man. She always attempted to please and to avoid sharing her true feelings whenever a problem arose.

When she was eleven years old, her mother had developed terminal cancer. Her father had asked her to come home early from school each day and be a caretaker for her mother until he arrived home. She had not been permitted to attend any school activities or play with children her age. She had been frightened and worried about her mother at this time and had been given a responsibility beyond her age. In spite of all her hard work and efforts to help, her mother had died. Debra had felt that she was a failure and had felt guilty about her occasional desires to be doing other things instead of caring for her mother. She had begun at that time to feel unworthy of being cared for.

As she remembered these events, she was drawn back to an even earlier set of memories. When she was very young, her mother had expressed dismay over the circumstances of Debra's birth, saying that at the time "there was no room for a baby." That message had permeated Debra's being and had reappeared once she was pregnant with her own first child. She interpreted her mother's statement as meaning that her mother had not wanted her. In reality, her family had been one of several families living in a small home under crowded conditions, and there had indeed been "no room for a baby," but there was no indication that Debra had not been wanted.

At this point, Debra's unconscious working model about what was happening in the middle of her pregnancy was derived from what she had picked up as a very young infant. This misperception and identification with her child-self was being re-created in her current pregnancy. In therapy, she was able to reframe this early life experience by imagining the joy that her mother experienced in being pregnant, being able to start a new life with her husband. Even though circumstances were difficult, it was no doubt her concern for the baby having all that she needed that made her worry about their situation. After three therapeutic visits, Debra was able to talk to her husband about the support she needed, express her grief about her mother, release her younger child-self from carrying the burden of guilt for her mother's death, and identify with the joy that her mother had felt when she was pregnant with Debra. She began to nurture herself, her appetite improved, and she visualized the baby growing and developing. After a short time the baby grew rapidly, and Debra delivered a healthy, full-term infant weighing eight pounds and seven ounces. Her perception of her infant and their first weeks together were significantly changed by this added support.

In another situation we encountered a young woman, Colleen, who was experiencing anxiety during her thirty-second week of pregnancy. Her midwife suggested she talk with a therapist about her anxiety. Her second pregnancy was progressing normally, but she was concerned about how to cut down her workload to accommodate breast-feeding and give herself time to recuperate and be with her baby after the birth. As she continued expressing her concerns, she began to experience tension in the uterus and contractions. She became frightened. The therapist asked her to allow herself to let those feelings take her to a deeper level of inner focus and to drift back to when these feelings began.

She quickly saw herself in her mind's eye in the midwife's office a few days earlier when she had been informed that she was showing some sugar in her urine, and the midwife had suggested further evaluation by her obstetrician. The obstetrician had suggested that the sugar could probably be controlled by diet but that if not, insulin would be necessary. She now realized that it was at that moment that she had become very fearful. She remembered that she had a terror of needles, a terror that had begun when she was a young child, having been held down as a toddler while a cut was sewn up and again while sutures were removed. Using mental imagery, she was able to redo in her mind that childhood experience in a way that enabled her to feel in control. She also learned how to imagine that her arm was numb. This enabled her to release the past trauma and learn how to use this self-anesthesia for any future injections if necessary.

Once she had worked through her needle phobia, she was able to feel more confident and relaxed, and the uterine contractions stopped. She had not realized until that time the power of her unconscious to affect her body. Although Colleen had initially talked about her current workload as a cause of anxiety, it was only with a deeper level of exploration that she discovered the earlier trauma. This earlier event had been unresolved and had not come up until her pregnancy, when the thought of needles elicited a strong fear that emerged as a projection onto the pregnancy. She was pleased to learn relaxation techniques to help reduce tension that might arise in the future. She was also helped to visualize a future successful pregnancy and full-term birth, which she experienced two months later.

Sometimes during pregnancy a mother will express concern about the stress she is experiencing in her life and about how this stress might affect the baby in utero. It has been documented that fetal heartbeat increases when mothers are extremely anxious, but it is important to recognize that some stress is a normal part of human life and adjustment and that babies can also adapt to the variations of maternal behavior and intrauterine life. Thus, fetuses do just fine in this normal adaptation. Severe, chronic maternal stress and anxiety, on the other hand, needs to be addressed, and mothers need help and support to relieve this condition. Any mother who is feeling unusual stress might give herself permission to take some quiet time to release tension and to explore what might be causing the stress.

An inward focus is one of the most universal psychological changes in pregnancy, and Winnicott described this beautifully.[9] A pregnant woman "will always say her interest gradually narrows down. Perhaps it is better to say that the direction of her interest turns from outward to inward. She slowly but surely comes to believe that the center of the world is in her own body."

Thailand offers an interesting example of the way the adjustment is handled outside the United States. For centuries Thai mothers, upon becoming pregnant, have purchased a clay statue of a mother and infant. At the time of birth the statue is thrown into the river; thus, the image of the mother and infant before birth is literally destroyed, to be replaced by the reality.

FATHERS

Prospective fathers go through an upheaval that is similar to that of the mothers. Pregnancy is a period when they must extend and reevaluate their own roles as providers to the family, role models for the new child, and supporters of their wives, who are going through their own major readjustment. Fathers draw naturally on their experience with their own fathers, although not always with satisfactory effect. As a complicating factor, in the nuclear family structure typical to the United States, a young father is often the only support for his wife when they no longer live within comfortable geographic or psychological distance of their relatives. In addition, fathers also have concerns and needs that may affect how they handle the pregnancy.

Fathers have few supports to help them adjust to a more active role with their wives and babies. This is most unfortunate because today the majority of new fathers are eager to do their part, and this valuable energy for bonding needs to be captured. Years ago, the anthropologist Margaret Mead realized the potential power of the father–infant bond: "No developing society that needs men to leave home and do his 'thing' for the society ever allows young men in to handle or touch their newborns. There's always a taboo against it. For they know somewhere that, if they did, the new fathers would become so 'hooked' that they would never get out and do their 'thing' properly." [10] In our lonely, nuclear families a father's best "thing" is to become more involved with his wife and new baby. If the obstetrician, midwife, or pediatrician directs some questions to the future father at a prenatal visit, the father's self-esteem will be enhanced. This recognition may increase his enthusiasm for the vital role he will play during labor and after the baby arrives.

What was once a transitional period with carefully worked out traditions for support has become a time of crisis with no societal mechanisms for helping expectant parents cope with the profound changes and developmental conflicts. As we mentioned earlier, in isolated, small families in the United States a woman and, especially, a man may not be acquainted with babies or prospective parents and, although expecting a baby, may not be able to discuss or visit with anyone else involved with pregnancy.

THE EFFECT OF NEW TECHNOLOGY ON DEVELOPING BONDS

The use of amniocentesis and ultrasound has affected parents' perceptions in a variety of ways. The tests often have beneficial results by removing some of the anxiety about the possibility of any abnormality. We have seen that parents sometimes name their baby after an ultrasound examination is done, and they often carry around the picture of the very small fetus. On the other hand, parents have discussed with us the disappointment they experienced when they discovered the sex of the baby—half of the mystery was over.

For the last two decades an intense effort has been mounted to test the normality of the fetus using ever more sophisticated screening procedures. These include the ultrasound imaging of the fetus, a blood test for alpha-feto-protein to detect several problems including abnormalities of the spine and central nervous system, and tests for Down syndrome and other conditions. Recently, two hormonal tests have been added to this procedure. In a large percentage of cases, the results from the various tests just mentioned show a normal fetus, and the tests thus have helped reassure many mothers about their babies. Yet, at the same time, the tests have also temporarily caused unnecessary anxiety, because the initial screening findings sometimes suggest an abnormality that is subsequently not confirmed with further testing. For instance, with the initial testing of 1,000 pregnant women, 30 mothers may be found to have a possible problem. These mothers naturally become extremely anxious, despite the fact that 29 mothers out of the 30 will be found on further testing to have a normal infant.[11] Thus, to find 1 abnormal baby (with Down syndrome or a back malformation) among 1,000 babies, 29 women may be frightened for a week or so until more fine-grained testing reassures them. Also, in spite of this reassurance, 1 to 2 of these 29 mothers and fathers continue to believe that their baby is not quite right even though they have been told several times that their baby is normal.

Although television and newspaper reports about malformed children abound, it is reassuring to appreciate that abnormalities are relatively rare. Among 100 babies, 1 to 2 major abnormalities occur, and a number of these can be treated surgically. It has always been common during pregnancy for mothers to have fantasies as well as fears and sometimes very scary dreams. In fact, most mothers dream about having an abnormal baby. However, mothers' fears have probably been overaccentuated by many new tests to rule out various malformations.

When a mother is concerned about the health of her baby during pregnancy or afterward and the medical findings are normal, it is helpful for the caregivers to explore with the mother what this fear might represent or symbolize. Often only a modest amount of exploration is required to resolve these disturbing feelings. A rather typical instance of the way such fears develop can be seen in the following incidents from our practice.

Becky complained to her pediatrician that she believed there was something wrong with her six-month-old girl, and she did not feel close to her. Although her pediatrician discussed with her how normal the baby acted, her new baby, Bridgette, just did not seem okay to Becky. She said Bridgette was quiet and passive compared to her active three-year-old boy.

Becky's pregnancy had been planned, but during the first trimester, she had experienced bleeding, and bed rest had been ordered for three weeks. After this three-week period the pregnancy had been normal, labor and birth had been normal, and she had delivered a healthy girl. Her fear about Bridgette actually had begun during the three weeks of bed rest, when she had begun to wonder if the baby was really normal. When fetal movement had begun, Becky had observed that the movements were much less frequent and strong than in her previous pregnancy, a fact that reinforced her concern, which she had not expressed to anyone.

Despite the healthy, full-term birth, Becky could not rid herself of the fear that the baby was in some way damaged because of something wrong with her own body. As a sensitive caregiver listened to her fears, Becky gradually realized that she had been holding this fear since early in pregnancy, had felt guilty about her own body's capacities, and had been afraid to express it to anyone. Bringing this to the light of day, she began the process of healing. While it would have been healthier and easier if her fears could have been alleviated much sooner in the pregnancy, she was able to relinquish them when their source became clear. Only when her feelings were heard could Becky "take in" the doctor's information that this baby simply had a very different temperament, and that her original concerns were unfounded. If a mother has persistent concerns, worries, or symptoms, the sooner these can be discussed, the better chance a woman has for a relaxed and confident time during pregnancy.

As the pregnancy progresses, other technological assessments are used to evaluate the fetus's growth and development, the fetus's adaptive physiology, and the placenta's ability to transfer adequate nutrients and oxygen to the fetus and remove carbon dioxide. At this time, the interpretation of some of these tests has not been completely developed and refined. Many couples have been frightened by questionable results.

How should couples manage this testing to avoid unnecessary anxiety? First, they should ask questions, particularly, "Are these results definite?" In one parent group, several mothers and fathers emphasized that the only way they managed was by asking questions repeatedly. At the end of a meeting with expectant parents in which we have given an explanation of a problem or interpretation of an ill-defined screening result, we have found it necessary to ask the parents to explain in their own words how they see the situation (for example: "Maybe you can explain to me how you see the problem" or "Maybe you can tell me what you understand from what I have been telling you"). In our work with parents, we realize that sometimes we go too quickly or use complicated language. We have been impressed at how often parents have misunderstood or become so frightened that they have been afraid to ask questions.

A particular burden of anxiety is laid on expectant parents who have been involved for several years in the complicated but advancing technological approach to infertility. This involves long ordeals of sperm counts, rectal temperature plots, gynecological exploration, surgery for the wife or for varicocele in the husband, artificial insemination, and in vitro fertilization. Powerful drugs that have psychological side effects are used. When the woman is finally pregnant, she and her partner experience elation and anxiety, hope and fear, eager anticipation and caution. Only when pregnancy is well under way do they begin to relax enough to feel a bit more confident.

Parents who have been physically and emotionally ravaged by the cycles of infertility treatment often have unexpressed concerns about their inadequacies and hidden fears about a possible defect in their baby. Often the mothers require both continual support and confirmation that the pregnancy is progressing satisfactorily. Parents who have had many losses such as miscarriages and stillbirths in their attempt to have a baby must expect to experience a long period of grief. Often group work or therapy can help them complete their reactions and enable them to deal with the new baby in a reasonably satisfactory fashion. If their grief is incompletely resolved, they run the risk of saddling their new baby with many of the concerns and worries they have been carrying about the lost baby. This can result in overconcern and overprotection toward the new, healthy baby.

RECOMMENDATIONS

1. *Staying in touch with each other.* Expectant parents should do their best to find time to talk with each other about what lies ahead. Pregnancy in some women and men stirs up issues that previously appeared to be settled. Talking together at least two or three times a week will enable the father and mother to find out how each is feeling, and this will be enriching and reassuring to both.

2. *History.* Early in pregnancy it is important for parents to supply the physician and nurse with information about what diseases are in the family and about any abortions, stillbirths, neonatal deaths or illnesses, and experiences with previous pregnancies and births. If these issues or other deep-seated worries come to mind frequently and appear not to be settled completely, the expectant parents would be wise to find a psychotherapist who could help them bring these issues to rest.

3. *Resolving problems.* Certain medical conditions such as premature labor and severe vomiting requiring hospitalization have been managed and, in some cases, alleviated using psychotherapy and hypnosis. With these techniques the woman can understand the origin of her problem and may sometimes be able to resolve it. Self-hypnosis can be learned in just a few visits. Of course, this is done concurrently with medical checkups.

4. *Labor support.* Parents might consider arranging for continuous support during labor. Continuous emotional support from an experienced woman (doula) has been shown to decrease significantly the length of labor, the incidence of cesarean sections, and other complications of labor. Every couple should consider making arrangements early in the third trimester to find a woman experienced at providing labor support in their community. Doulas of North America (DONA), 1100 23rd Avenue East, Seattle, WA 98112, FAX (206) 325-5098, will help couples find a doula in their area. Childbirth educators can also usually tell you who is available in your community. In addition to the obstetric benefits, both mothers and fathers who have had a doula report enthusiastically about the emotional advantages to them, both individually and to their marriage. In Chapters 2 and 4 we provide further descriptions of what a doula does and how this fits with the role of the partner.

5. *Prenatal classes.* We strongly support the availability of the prenatal classes in which parents can share with each other, as well as with other couples, their many individual experiences, concerns, needs, and questions. These classes offer time to mull over and appreciate how many of their worries are a normal part of pregnancy. An important component is the opportunity to receive up-to-date information from a childbirth educator. The friendships the expectant mother and father form with the members in these groups help them not only through the critical months of pregnancy but also in the adjustment to the newborn and to breast-feeding. One of the great benefits of childbirth education classes in the community, in contrast to those sponsored by a hospital, has been the opportunity for expectant parents to hear about the variety of childbirth options available and to choose what seems best for them. Although the stated purpose of these groups is to prepare parents for the actual labor and birth, another important result is the sharing of hopes, expectations, fears, and questions. New friends partly substitute for an extended family and help with the adjustment to the newborn. The ties made through shared participation are strong, and couples will often stay in touch with each other for years afterward.

6. *Tours.* Almost all hospitals have regularly scheduled tours of the labor and delivery area and the postpartum divisions. Parents usually welcome this advance view of the environment where their new baby will be born, and the opportunity to ask questions about exactly what will happen is particularly valuable.

7. *Cesarean birth.* Mothers who are facing cesarean childbirth should have detailed preparation about the procedures involved. The presence of fathers in the operating room and closer contact between mothers and newborns appear to improve developing family ties, the "birth" of the families. In hospitals where family-centered maternity care has been extended to cesarean births, there is no evidence of harm to any of those involved, only benefits. When the father is with the mother, there should be detailed preparation about what to expect in the operating room. The father should stay at the mother's head area, holding her hand and saying simple words of reassurance, such as, "I love you and everything is going to be fine." This is not a time for a "photographic essay." The next day the doula and the father should review the experience with the mother to clarify and correct any misconceptions about what went on and to reassure the mother that she did the best she could.

8. *Unusual stress.* Major stresses in the family such as a serious illness or the death of a close relative (e.g., father or mother, brother or sister, or husband) can have a disturbing influence on the pregnancy, early maternal caretaking, and affectionate interaction with the young infant. By being aware of the impact of these stresses, parents can often prevent or alleviate potential problems and anxiety.

9. *Extended hospitalization.* When pregnant women require hospitalization in high-risk obstetrical care centers for prolonged periods as a result of conditions such as toxemia, diabetes, hypertension, and intrauterine growth retardation, it is necessary to adapt the hospital setting and encourage family support within hospital guidelines. The woman and her husband should ask about visiting policies for their other children, extra beds for fathers-to-be to room overnight with their wives, and special dining rooms for the family to eat together. Parents can press for these and other alterations to make the hospital more homelike.

2

LABOR AND BIRTH

To understand the tie between a mother and father and their newborn, we must examine the care that the parents, and especially the mother, receive during the critical period of labor and birth. Some people say that although birth is important, it is only one day in a person's life. Others see birth as a significant moment in development. Some even see the experience of birth as the most influential moment of life for the baby and the mother, and often for the father. We see birth as highly significant, but not as an isolated experience. A number of factors, including the woman's past experience, her present life situation, and the hospital setting, converge to shape these few hours and determine their influence on development.

Years after having a child, women remember if they felt in

control or out of control when giving birth; if they were treated respectfully and felt validated; if they felt ignored, put down, or inadequate; or if they felt deprived of choices or invaded by many interventions. They remember each negative or positive word spoken to them. They remember if their partner was truly with them emotionally during labor rather than involved in other activities, and if a caretaker was present just for them or if they and their partner were left alone for any length of time. They recall many years later if they were able to hold their infant immediately after birth or were separated for long periods of time.[1] Sometimes it is not possible fully to resolve experiences, beliefs, or expectations that a woman brings with her to labor and birth. Caregivers can, however, help plan a birth to be as meaningful, uncomplicated, and empowering as possible for the mother and the father, and as healthy as possible for the newborn.[2]

The female human body is fully prepared to give birth, and the system works well when the woman is relaxed and is helped to let her body do what it knows how to do. Relaxation, mind–body visualizations (just like ones that many Olympic athletes use), emotional support, and other techniques can help this process. Both parents also need basic knowledge about the possible interventions that may become necessary or may be offered. They can then draw up a birth plan to discuss with their obstetrician or midwife ahead of time to be sure she or he is in complete agreement. The concurrence of the backup caregiver, should the chosen one not be available, is also vital.

DEVELOPING AND FOLLOWING A BIRTH PLAN

As an example of a typical experience, the following narrative is based on a number of cases in the authors' practice.

Planning for their first baby, Patricia and Jim found a doctor who was interested in working with them on a birth plan. The couple had read a great deal and had definite ideas and hopes for their child's birth. For example, Pat wanted to be able to walk during labor for as long as possible to allow gravity and body position to help facilitate contractions and the descent of the baby. The doctor agreed to check the fetal heartbeat only every fifteen minutes instead of using continuous monitoring, which would have compelled Patricia to stay mostly in bed. The doctor believed that most of their ideas made sense for the normal course of labor, and the three of them agreed that they would certainly go along with their doctor's medical decisions if there was any cause for concern.

The doctor agreed wholeheartedly with them that a labor support person (a doula) was a wonderful idea. Patricia and Jim interviewed some women they had heard about through their childbirth education class. After choosing their doula, they met with her for three visits before the birth and learned and practiced physical relaxation exercises, visualizations, position changes for labor, and some alternative positions for the birth itself, such as a supported semisquatting position.

In their discussions, Patricia talked about some of her fears about pain. She learned from the doula how to mentally erase non-helpful comments from others, such as "Labor is so painful" and concentrate more on her body's power and strength to birth a baby. They discussed Jim's feelings about labor and what role he would take in the support. The most important aspect for Patricia was that Jim should be her main support and not feel pushed aside by the more experienced caregivers. They talked about taking turns and working as a team. There was no competition here: the doula talked about being supportive to both of them, a helping relationship. During practice sessions on relaxation techniques, Patricia recognized that when she had an anxious thought, her muscles tensed. She learned, through breathing and imagery, to release the tension.

When labor began, their preparation turned out to be very valuable. The physical relaxation techniques (releasing tension from each group of muscles) turned out to be less helpful than they had thought, but breathing through the contractions and using mental visualizations markedly reduced the stress and pain of the labor. Patricia also found that her husband and the doula were almost ideal in giving her continuous support and guidance during labor. Rather surprisingly, after three and a half hours she delivered a healthy seven-and-a-half-pound boy and she had only a minor tear and no episiotomy. They both felt that all the preparation had proved worthwhile.

The nurturing and support they received in labor gave them a deep sense of accomplishment and trust in them-selves. They had felt in control, respected, and thoughtfully supported. When holding their baby, they experienced an overwhelming feeling of loving connection. It is our impression and experience that the more the parents are cared for in labor, the more easily they are able to take in their baby, begin to build a tie, and sense their baby's needs.

Unfortunately, not all deliveries go so smoothly. Certain unavoidable circumstances can change the course. Other events, such as those that follow, are avoidable with cooperation between the parents and the medical staff.

Mary had started contractions, which were occurring every five minutes. She called her medical caregiver and was told to come to the hospital. A short time after arriving at the hospital, the contractions slowed down and became sporadic. The obstetrician believed he had a choice either of having her go home and seeing if the contractions would pick up again, or rupturing her membranes and seeing if labor would pick up. Since she was at term and already in the hospital and it appeared that her labor was beginning, he decided to rupture the membranes. Several hours later, the contractions had increased slightly in frequency, but they were not forceful and there was no change in the dilation of the cervical opening.

At this point, the obstetrician decided to start an oxytocin drip (oxytocin is a natural hormone that stimulates labor). He gradually increased the oxytocin, but with little change in the dilation. As the dose was increased, the contractions became strong and quite painful. Although Mary had planned not to have any pain medication, her distress was much more than she had expected and she requested an epidural. Even though she had planned to keep walking around, she was now confined to bed with the epidural and the intravenous oxytocin infusion. Progress was slow and the labor long. As time passed, Mary and her husband become more and more discouraged and exhausted.

As the labor approached twenty hours, the obstetrician mentioned that due to the rupture of the membranes it would be essential to get the baby out before twenty-four hours. At this time, Mary was noted to have a fever. A review of her temperature chart showed a gradual increase over the preceding eight hours. Though this could have been due to the epidural analgesia, the obstetrician was concerned that the fever could have been due to an infection, which might affect the infant. He returned and told the parents about this. At that time he said that, given this risk, it might be safer to do a cesarean section. This drastically changed all of the parents' plans, but everyone's concern was to produce a normal healthy baby and to maintain the mother's health.

A cesarean delivery was performed without problems, but the baby at birth had rapid respiration. This triggered a call to a neonatologist to look at the baby. She assured the parents that they had a healthy infant, but that it would be necessary for the baby to go to a special area for observation and to undergo a blood culture and spinal tap because of the possibility that the breathing difficulty and the mother's temperature were due to infection. This resulted in separation of mother and baby. Although Mary was given permission to visit the baby in the nursery, the discomfort from her cesarean section and her headache from the epidural held her back until the following morning when she was taken to the baby, who by this time was improved but was still in an isolette. Mary was allowed to hold the baby, but due to her discomfort and the rather public situation in the nursery, she did not wish to start her breast-feeding at that time. She was discouraged about this because she had planned for many weeks to breast feed and to hold her baby immediately after birth, as she had seen on a video-tape.

What happened to Mary occurs more often than necessary in the United States today. The mother may anticipate that every-thing will go very smoothly and that she will not need any addi-tional support or any advance planning because she has an obstetrician with an excellent reputation. Certain interventions used to speed up the labor or to control the delivery and, in part, override the normal physiological mechanism do need discussion in advance and careful decision making.

Although Mary was having contractions, she was not in labor by most definitions, since she was not dilating and there was no thinning of the cervix or bloody show, and she had not sponta-neously ruptured her membranes. In retrospect, she was probably not ready to go into active labor, and she would have been better off by going home and waiting for real labor to begin. If she had prepared a birth plan together with her obstetrician—specifying that, barring unusual circumstances, there would be no rupturing of the membranes, no monitoring, and no oxytocin—she might have had the chance to make a choice. She might have been able to go home until active labor began. There she could have walked around the house, been with her husband, and come back when labor had really started. In such a case, the cesarean section and the epidural might not have been necessary.

Each technological intervention needs to be weighed not only for its intrinsic risks and benefits but also for its effect on the birth experience and, therefore, on the first encounter between parent and child. Since one intervention also leads to another, the options they open or close for the laboring mother also need to be considered. They can take on a life of their own. One intervention

causes the next one to be needed and eventually leads to a cascade of interventions of increasing seriousness.

EFFECTS OF MEDICAL INTERVENTIONS

In our 1993 book, *Mothering the Mother*, we examined in detail the effects on the cesarean rate and the birth experience of each type of medical intervention.[3] A brief summary follows.

Rupture of Membranes

If a mother is in labor, artificial rupture of the membranes decreases the total length of labor by about 40 to 120 minutes.[4] However, the procedure starts a time clock that is usually allowed only twenty-four hours to run before delivery of the infant is required because of concern about bacteria invading the uterus and infecting the fetus. The intact membranes also provide a barrier during labor that cushions the baby's head. As the head descends through the birth canal, a certain number of babies suffer a hemorrhage between the scalp and the bones of the skull. This is called a "cephalohematoma" and is more common when there is no cushioning bag of waters to protect the head during active labor. This is not a dangerous complication, has no aftereffects, and requires no treatments, but it does upset parents. Lastly, the procedure of rupturing the membranes can be painful, and mothers find it uncomfortable.

Many mothers have told us that they tend to lose control of their labor after the rupture. The sense of a natural, manageable sequence of events is lost, and the mother may feel more helpless. It is our own opinion that it is best not to rupture the membranes, unless there is a special medical need.

Fetal Monitoring

Another major decision for the parents and the obstetrician is whether there should be routine monitoring of the fetal heart rate. Nine separate studies throughout the world have not shown any improvement in outcome for the baby with monitoring of healthy women.[5] In spite of this, fetal monitoring is commonly used throughout the United States to reduce the threat of a lawsuit in case there is any problem with the baby. Continuous monitoring prevents a mother from walking around during most of the labor. Therefore, it decreases the effect of gravity and often lengthens the labor. In all the nine studies of monitoring, the number of cesarean deliveries was doubled in the group that was monitored. In most delivery units, the mother has some flexibility about the monitoring. If a mother is healthy and the baby is doing well, she can labor without the monitor and have the fetal heart rate checked with a stethoscope every ten to fifteen minutes or have a short monitor strip obtained every half hour or hour. Most experts who have investigated the subject believe that in women without any complications and with normal growth and development of the fetus, monitoring offers no advantage.

Oxytocin/Pitocin

A third intervention involves the natural hormone oxytocin, which is often used to augment the strength and frequency of contractions. (Pitocin is a brand name of oxytocin.) The usual practice is to increase the dose until the contractions have significantly intensified. Mothers who have been able to manage the discomfort of normal labor contractions up to this point, or in previous labors, often find the augmented pains so intense that they may feel forced to go against their initial plan to avoid medication. The usual medication administered in this situation is a continuous epidural infusion. With the use of oxytocin, some mothers develop such severe contractions of the uterus that it must be discontinued and a counteracting medication must be administered. Many mothers have reported never being able to get on top of the contractions because they were so painful and continuous.

Epidural Analgesia

Epidural analgesia is a frequently used method of pain control that successfully numbs the pain of contractions for most mothers. However, in some situations the sensation of the contractions still causes enough pain to be extremely uncomfortable. Mothers' experiences with epidural analgesia have been mixed.[6] There is a significant increase in cesarean-section deliveries among mothers who have epidurals. This is often related to the inability of the mother to feel the natural urge to push in the second stage of labor.

Unfortunately, when women receive an epidural early in labor, one-third of them and their infants develop a fever up to as high as 103 degrees to 104 degrees.[7] The fetal temperature is normally six-tenths of a degree higher than the mother's. When these infants are delivered, the physician cannot determine whether the mother's and the infant's elevated temperatures are the result of an infection or just an artifact of the mother's epidural. Therefore, the infant is placed in an isolette and requires a spinal-tap culture and a blood culture and has to receive antibiotics until his or her cultures show no infection (usually three days). In addition, about 25 percent of babies whose mothers have an epidural often have difficulty in quickly, easily, and smoothly catching on to breast-feeding. Some mothers also feel that they have been deprived of the birth experience because they cannot feel their baby emerge, and they do not have a sense of control over their labor or a sense of accomplishment. Epidurals may partially prevent the release of oxytocin that normally occurs at birth and that influences a mother's feelings toward her baby.

Cesarean Section

Cesarean delivery is obviously needed in certain situations and has saved many lives. However, physicians agree that surgery is associated with increased rates of illness among both mothers and babies, as well as with higher infant and maternal mortality. Therefore, we have long cast our vote against elective cesarean sections, or any that could possibly be avoided. A cesarean delivery is major abdominal surgery, is extremely painful, and requires a month or more of recuperation time for the mother. These effects are greatest at the time when she has planned to be fully available to her new baby.

Episiotomy

Lastly, a mother-to-be and her obstetrician need to discuss episiotomies. An episiotomy can create such discomfort for the mother that it inhibits her ability to manage her baby easily in the first days of life. Studies on a large number of women by Klein and others[8] have shown that episiotomies actually promote more extensive, large tears in the vaginal opening where the episiotomy is made. These are associated with prolonged discomfort and a longer time to heal in this area than the more natural small tears that often heal naturally when left alone. An episiotomy can be disabling for several weeks after delivery. As an alternative to episiotomy, the delivery of the head can be carefully controlled. Warm compresses, along with oil, can be placed over the perineum so that the mother feels little pain. When this is done, there is usually only a small separation or break in the surface mucosa that requires a few stitches. Such a break is not as bothersome to the mother in the postnatal period, and it knits together quickly and naturally.

With the short hospital stays that are now typical, cesarean- and episiotomy-related problems are intensified. The pain of an episiotomy and the pain and systemic reaction to major abdominal surgery following cesarean deliveries are even more debilitating and disruptive to the mother when she finds herself at home on her own or with a partner who is also a new parent.

EMOTIONAL SUPPORT DURING LABOR

We strongly believe that the one way markedly to reduce problems and interventions in obstetrics is for a mother or a couple to have complete and continuous emotional support. If the midwife or the hospital staff do not provide this, the couple can hire their own doula in the last months of pregnancy, develop with her their own birth plan, and have her available to help the couple or mother continuously through labor and delivery. Another advantage of continuous emotional support is the underlying message to the woman of her value as a person, and as a mother and future caregiver. No matter what procedures she goes through, when she feels completely validated, her belief in her own competence can be sustained and can resonate throughout her whole life.

Evidence from a number of sources reveals that the extent of the emotional and physical support that a mother receives in labor becomes a metaphor for how she visualizes herself and how she feels as she begins to care for her own baby. The kind of support that we are describing can be provided by any nurturing caregiver with experience in childbirth: a nurse, midwife, or doula.[9]

The major work of a doula, which we describe in our book *Mothering the Mother*,[10] is to create a "holding" environment for the woman in labor in which the mother can be emotionally as well as physically supported, without any interruption. This feeling of safety with another woman creates a kind of inner strength that enables a woman to begin to test the limits of her own capacities and to experience dimensions possibly not recognized before—or perhaps recognized but not risked. This freedom to be one's true self generates feelings of empowerment, of creativity. As a new mother quoted in our book said to one doula, "Your staying with me all the time and your total support, at the same time trusting me completely, gave me a sense of knowing that I was strong enough to handle anything in my life."

As she prepares to move through the major developmental changes associated with experiencing labor and delivery and with becoming a parent, a woman is unusually dependent and open. She also needs the freedom to turn in to herself—to take charge at an instinctual level in response to what her body wants to do. There is a paradox here: A woman in labor needs total support—in order to let go completely, to allow her own system to adapt and respond to the power of the birthing process. This mixed need can be confusing to the mother herself and may be difficult for others to appreciate. Often caregivers find it hard to understand this balance.

In certain situations, the continuous emotional support may have a deeper therapeutic effect. During birth there is a psychological regression to a woman's own birth, to her essential vulnerability. If a woman has had inadequate or inappropriate mothering herself, the nurturing provided during this unique period may help to "remother" the mother and bring some degree of healing to that earlier experience. For this effect to occur, the caregiver attending a laboring woman needs special skills and insights. She must be comfortable with giving of herself and not afraid to love. She must be able to enter a mother's space and be highly responsive and aware of her needs, moods, changes, and unspoken feelings. At the same time, she needs to be flexible in this process, adapting herself to each mother's needs without trying to control or smother. In a real sense she "mothers the mother" and in this sense is always accepting and nonjudgmental. This feeling of total acceptance will remain with the mother as she relates to her own baby.

All mothers, and fathers, need emotional support and help during labor. Much of this support they can provide to each other. The mother needs to feel the father's caring, love, and sense of sharing in the intimate experience of bringing their child into the world. The father has a strong desire to help, to participate, to feel useful and active, and to feel important and necessary for the mother. But when two people share an emotional bond and an ongoing relationship, it is very difficult for a companion to remain continuously objective, calm, and removed to some degree from the mother's discomfort, fears, or dangers. In most cases—and this cannot be stated too often—the father will have the unexpressed but deeply felt question, Will everything be all right? Also, a father often has had little or no experience with the birth process.

For these reasons, every woman in labor needs not only the father but also a nurturing, experienced person who can calmly and skillfully help her cope with labor and be a reassuring and constant presence for both her and the father. As Illustration 1 indicates, an experienced doula, midwife, or nurse will offer a woman in labor total support in order for her to let go completely. This level of support is different from that of a person who is intimately related to the woman in labor. These two kinds of support complement each other. A midwife, nurse, or doula can help a woman work with her labor and guide her on how to stay relaxed and comfortable at home until labor is well established. She can reassure the pregnant woman that she will have the ability and confidence to be an advocate on her own behalf. In the hospital she can help the father or other support person be less anxious, and she can serve as a role model for the less experienced person.

Very often the couple worry that an outside support person will take over and control the labor experience, as many individuals providing labor assistance have traditionally done. An experienced doula, midwife, or nurse will instead offer quiet reassurance and enhancement of the laboring woman's natural abilities, and she will remain aware that the couple will carry the memory of this experience throughout their lives. Such support also means encouraging and instructing the father on how he can best help and support the mother.

The mother gains more assured, steady emotional support

from her husband if he is less worried about what he is supposed to do and if they both can relax and trust the doula's expert care. A laboring woman's rapid change of mood may alarm an inexperienced father or a partner and compound the mother's fears. "If you leave the mother alone for even five minutes," a doula once commented to us, "she begins to become distressed. She begins to fall apart and lose control, and when you return, it may take a half hour to get her settled down."

Even experienced fathers, believing that their wives in labor are doing fine, may not recognize underlying needs or fears. One second-time father thought his wife's labor was going well and brought his radio into the labor room to hear a cherished football game. She reported later how abandoned she had felt and said that she somehow could not tell him because she "was supposed to know how to do it." With their first baby, he had been readily available to her and involved. In relating the story, she realized that one obstetrical nurse had stayed with them through the whole first birth, but that with the second birth, no personnel had been around. "Perhaps they thought we could handle it ourselves—and we did, too. I was so upset that I felt depressed for many weeks afterward." Another woman had a friend as her "labor coach." This woman "took over" the management of the labor, believing sincerely that she was providing the best support. The mother later revealed that she had wanted to do the labor differently but had been worried about hurting her friend's feelings. In such a situation a doula or other trained birth assistant might have been able to help both of them organize differently around the labor by encouraging the mother to express and clarify her own wishes and find ways to validate and incorporate the partner's ideas and desire to help.

As we pointed out in *Mothering the Mother,*[11] this kind of continuous emotional support has highly significant obstetrical advantages. The results of seven randomized trials, when calculated together, reveal that the presence of a doula reduces the overall cesarean rate by 50 percent, the length of labor by 25 percent, oxytocin use by 40 percent, pain-medication use by 30 percent, the need for forceps by 40 percent, and requests for epidurals by 60 percent.

It is assumed that a midwife, childbirth nurse, or doula will be a woman, and several advantages probably account for this. A mother in labor can usually be less inhibited in the presence of another woman. The intimate aspects of bodily function are more easily expressed with a person of the same gender. In addition, the softer, quieter, gentler, sensitive, nurturing qualities of "mothering" have traditionally come from women in our culture.

For the actual delivery, medical caregivers are in charge. A doula remains by the mother's side along with the father, while a nurse, a midwife, or an obstetrician helps with the delivery. Afterward, everyone involved congratulates the parents, and especially the new mother, on their accomplishment.

Ideally, the day after the delivery, a doula or a nurse will visit with the family and ask them what they remember about the birth and whether they have any questions or concerns. It is important for parents to discuss the birth experience, to share all their positive feelings and, if appropriate, their negative feelings. Also, almost all mothers gain from hearing details that fill in many of the missing pieces of the experience for them, because they can gain a new perception of their own participation. Often mothers feel they failed to perform well and did not do something right. A retelling of the birth story helps them understand what actually went on during their labor and delivery. It is an opportunity to heighten the mother's self-image by pointing out the strength she showed and the way her body followed an age-old biological course. If complications occurred, the mother can be helped to integrate and sometimes reframe the experience.

EFFECTS OF EMOTIONAL SUPPORT ON MATERNAL BEHAVIOR AND ATTITUDE

We have explored in depth this short but most significant time in a woman's life because the care in labor appears to affect a mother's attitudes, feelings, and responses to her family, herself, and especially her new baby, to a remarkable degree. In one study of such effects, both mothers without doula support and with doula support were interviewed immediately after delivery and six weeks later. Women who had doula support during labor had a heightened sense of self-esteem, believed they had coped well with labor, and thought the labor had been easier than they would have imagined. Women who received this support reported being less anxious twenty-four hours after birth than mothers without a doula. Doula-supported mothers were significantly less depressed at six weeks postpartum, as measured on a standard depression scale, than mothers who had had no doula. In addition, doula-supported mothers had a significantly greater incidence of breast-feeding without supplements and feeding on demand, and they breast-fed for a longer period of time.[12]

In our first doula study in Guatemala, we saw a hint of some of the effects. Through a one-way mirror we observed both groups of Guatemalan mothers with their babies in the first twenty-five minutes after leaving the delivery room in a standardized situation. The doula-assisted mothers showed more affectionate interaction with their infants, with more smiling, talking, and stroking than the mothers who did not have a doula.[13] Not only did the supported mothers have changed views of themselves, but they began to view their infants differently, too. In another study the supported mothers said it took them an average of 2.9 days to develop a relationship with their babies compared to 9.8 days for the nonsupported mothers. This feeling of attachment and readiness to fall in love with their babies made them less willing to leave their babies alone. They also reported picking up their babies more frequently when they cried than did nonsupported mothers.[14]

In this same study, the doula-supported mothers were more positive on all dimensions describing the specialness of their babies than were the nonsupported mothers. A higher percentage of supported mothers not only considered their babies beautiful, clever, healthy, and easy to manage but also believed their infants cried less than other babies. In fact, the supported mothers believed that their babies were "better" when compared to a "standard baby," whereas the nonsupported mothers perceived their babies as "almost as good as" or "not quite as good as" a "standard baby." "Support group mothers also perceived themselves as closer to their babies, as managing better, and as communicating better with their babies than control group mothers did," the study reported. A higher percentage of the doula-supported mothers reported that they were pleased to have their babies, found becoming a mother was easier than expected, and felt that they could look after their babies better than anyone else could. In contrast, the nonsupported mothers perceived their adaptation to motherhood as more difficult and felt that others could care for their baby as well as they could.

A most important aspect of emotional support in childbirth may be the most unexpected internalized one—that of the calm, nurturing, accepting, and holding model provided for the parents. Maternal care needs modeling; each generation benefits from the care received by the earlier one.

A mother of three-month-old twins recently told us about how a doula's care of her during labor has affected her care of her babies. When her labor was difficult, the doula consistently remained calm and caring. Now when her twins are upset, this mother finds herself staying calm, leaning on the example given by her doula. She commented, "I became aware that the way she was with me during labor is the way I am with the twins when they become upset, instead of freaking out and trying many things. They are able to calm down because I remain calm. In the past I would have been too worried about how to manage. It's like a contagious calm instead of contagious anxiety."

We hope that further studies support these very beneficial effects of support during labor. We believe emotional support is an essential ingredient for every laboring woman. It is needed to enhance not only the mother's physical and emotional health during childbirth but also the special relationship that ties the parents to each other and to their infant.

3

WHAT THE BABY BRINGS

A bonding relationship takes place between two people. To appreciate fully what can happen shortly after birth for the parents and the infant, we must describe not just the parents' experience but also the responsiveness and astonishing capacities of the infant in the first minutes, hours, and days of life.

NEWBORN STATES OF CONSCIOUSNESS

The key to our understanding begins with the work of two very patient observers of newborn infants, Heinz Prechtl[1] and Peter Wolff.[2] After unobtrusively recording newborn babies' every action, awake and asleep, over long periods of time throughout the day and night, they discovered that the normal behaviors of the infants were organized into six different states of consciousness. These six different ways of being in the world depend on the degree of wakefulness or sleep, and each of the states is accompanied by specific and individual behaviors.

By closely observing your own baby, you will soon learn to recognize the six states: the two sleep states—quiet sleep and active sleep—as well as the three awake states—quiet alert, active alert, and crying. The other state, drowsiness, is a transition between sleep and wakefulness.

One of the newborn's first responses after birth is to move into a quiet but alert state of consciousness. In this *quiet alert state,* which is very similar to the conscious attention we see in our friends when they are listening closely to us, babies rarely move. The baby's torso and arms mold to the parents' forms, the tiny hands touch the parents' skin, and the baby looks directly at the mother and father. In this state, newborns' eyes are wide open, bright and shiny, and they are especially fun to play with. They can follow a red ball, select pictures, and even imitate their mother's facial movements.

Right after birth, within the first hour of life, normal infants have a prolonged period of quiet alertness, averaging forty minutes, during which they look directly at their mother's and father's faces and eyes and can respond to voices.[3] It is as though newborns had rehearsed the perfect approach to the first meeting with their parents. (This may in fact be so; sleeping and waking states begin long before birth.) In this state, motor activity is suppressed, and all the baby's energy seems to be channeled into seeing, hearing, and responding.

During the first week of life, the normal baby spends about 10 percent of any twenty-four-hour day in this exciting and receptive state. Such alertness allows newborns to take in much of their surroundings and to respond and adapt to the environment. When your baby is in this state, you will see the first evidence of natural curiosity as the infant searches to understand the world. Illustrations 2 and 3 show babies in the quiet alert state shortly after birth.

During the *active alert state,* your baby is very different. The baby makes frequent movements and small sounds, and the eyes look about the room. This state appears when the baby is ready to eat or is fussy. Observations have shown that although the baby does not move continuously, there are episodes of movement that occur with a special rhythm. About every one to two minutes, a baby's arms, legs, body, or face will move. These movements may serve an adaptive purpose. Some scientists believe that they convey clues to parents about what their baby needs. Others believe that because these movements are interesting to watch, they may promote a natural interchange between parents and babies. Bursts of move-ment like this have been detected late in pregnancy in the fe-tus by placing sensitive measuring devices on the mother's abdomen.

The state called *drowsiness* usually occurs while the baby is waking up or falling asleep. The baby may continue to move, sometimes smiling, frowning, or pursing the lips. The eyes have a dull, glazed appearance and usually do not focus. The lids are droopy, and, just before closing, the eyes may roll upward.

In the *quiet sleep state,* a baby's face is relaxed, and the eyelids are closed and still. There are no body movements except rare startles and very, very fine mouth movements. In this state, infants are at full rest, and breathing is very regular as they take in the same amount of air with each breath.

In the *active sleep state,* an infant's eyes are usually closed, but occasionally they will flutter from closed to open. You can often see the eyes move under the lids. The term *rapid eye move-ment* (REM) sleep originated from the eye movements observed during this type of restless sleep. In active sleep, you will notice occasional body activity that ranges from movement of the baby's arms and legs to stirring of the entire body. Breathing is not regular and is slightly faster than in quiet sleep. While they remain asleep, infants in this state often make funny faces—grimaces, smiles, frowns—and may display chewing movements or bursts of sucking. When babies awake, they usually have been in active, rather than quiet, sleep. Adults experience such REM sleep when they are dreaming; no one knows whether infants also are dreaming in this particular sleep state.

During the newborn period, an infant sleeps most of the time—about 90 percent of the day or night—and often will fall asleep right at the breast. Half of this sleep time is spent in quiet sleep and the other half in active sleep. These two states alternate about every thirty minutes during sleep.

The *crying state,* an obvious way for infants to communicate, occurs when the baby is hungry or uncomfortable. Most mothers know that they can change babies' crying states by picking them up, soothing them, and putting them against their shoulder. The mothers who pick up their crying infants are giving them an opportunity not only to be quietly awake but also to learn about their world by scanning the room.

By recognizing the different states of consciousness and realizing when they occur and what the expected responses are in each, parents not only can get to know their infants but also can provide sensitively for their needs. For instance, when a baby is whimpering slightly and is stirring in active sleep, a parent who is aware that this occurs in thirty-minute cycles will not rush to feed or change the baby unless this gentle activity turns into the active awake or crying state. Once we understand and recognize the six patterns of newborn behavior, the mysterious world of newborns begins to make more sense.

AN INFANT'S SENSORY CAPACITIES

Vision

Mothers have long known that soon after birth their babies could see and respond visually to them. For a time, doctors were reluctant to believe them. However, thirty to forty years ago researchers discovered that mothers were right. They observed that when newborns in the quiet alert state were shown pictures, the infants looked at them and sometimes fixated on a photograph. The researchers could tell this occurred when they observed the reflection of the picture on the surface of the newborns' pupils.

Using this method, researchers learned that infants show preferences even among abstract patterns and are especially attracted to sharp outlines as well as light and dark contrasts. If infants find contrasting edges or contours, their eyes will scan in such a way as to provide maximum stimulation to the retina. Both eyes actually look in the direction of the pattern, and the baby shows attention not only by looking but also by lifting the upper eyelid, by "brightening" the eye, and by ceasing to suck.[4] Babies can also recognize color and are especially attracted to the human face.

The ability to see and focus on objects occurs mainly during the quiet alert state and thus can be missed by anyone not sensitive to the baby's cues. Another reason for our previous inability to recognize that newborns can see is related to the fact that they are born nearsighted and so cannot initially accommodate their vision to distances. Newborns' vision is best at a range of eight to ten inches from the face. Interestingly, this is about the same distance from which an infant views his mother's face during breast-feeding. If objects are moved too close or too far, they go out of focus and can be seen only as a blur. If parents want to test the infant's ability to focus and follow, they should keep objects in that eight-to ten-inch range. They should make sure that they have the baby's attention (the baby should be looking directly at the object) before they begin to move the object slowly.

When a moving object catches their attention, babies are apt to focus on it. They will follow it with their eyes and sometimes with their heads as well. If a red ball is moved slowly at a distance of ten inches from their face, they follow it first with their eyes and then turn their head horizontally and sometimes vertically. Initially, the babies' attention will be intense, but after a few minutes they lose some interest. They may turn away, and sometimes they become drowsy or actually fall asleep or "tune out" an apparently uninteresting image.

Investigators have discovered that newborns tend to scan the outer contours of patterns rather than look at inner details. Similarly, when babies look at other human faces, they usually scan the outline and then move to the eyes and mouth.[5] They find eyes particularly engrossing. Infants are active in their visual responses. When alert, babies look about spontaneously. They can even recognize depth and may respond with a defensive reaction to approaching objects. Babies prefer complexity, diversity, and movement, and they have visual memory.

Newborns also can process visual information, remember what they have seen, and use that information. If infants are shown the same picture for a long period of time, they tend to decrease their looking time, as if bored. However, if shown a new and different picture, they demonstrate renewed inter-est. This is called "response to novelty" and may signify an early ability to remember a picture already seen. Current evidence suggests that newborns can recognize their mothers and actually remember their faces. Feats of visual perception and memory by the baby indicate that the infant's visual talent is based not only on reflex eye movement but also on higher brain function.

In the quiet alert state, as the eyes become bright and widely open, infants will often stop moving or sucking and become very still. These short periods of rapt visual attention, occurring shortly after birth and throughout this early period, draw newborns into eye-to-eye contact, a vital element in human interaction. In this mutual gaze, the first dialogue begins; parents and children seem magnetically drawn into communication.

Hearing

Several months before birth, babies already have a well-developed ability to hear.[6] After birth they can distinguish between types of sound (e.g., a buzzer or a bell), loudness and pitch, different voices, familiar and unfamiliar sounds. They can even determine the direction from which sound is coming.

When a small bell is rung, infants will orient to the sound by first turning their eyes and then their heads in the direction of the sound. Orienting to sound is something humans do without thinking, and newborns start to do this from the first moments after birth; they look to the right when the sound is coming from the right and to the left when the sound is from the left. This ability to look toward the source of the sound may be part of the infants' attempts to get better reception, or this eye-and-ear response may be one of the many built-in connections between two or more senses—an adaptive response that ensures experiencing the environment as fully as possible.

Infants are most responsive to other human voices. Parents can have fun with their baby when she is in the quiet alert state by talking a short distance from one ear in a high-pitched voice. They may first notice the baby's eyes turning in the direction of their voices. Then, almost simultaneously, the baby's head will turn, her face will brighten, and her eyes will open a bit wider. Even more appealing to infants is being talked to and looked at simultaneously. Newborn babies prefer high-pitched voices, and mothers and fathers in many cultures seem instinctively to use high-pitched voices when they first talk to their babies after delivery. In a series of ingeniously designed studies, psychological researcher Anthony

DeCasper, from the University of North Carolina, discovered that newborns prefer hearing a woman's voice rather than a man's voice.[7] A newborn prefers the mother's voice over other women's voices, but in the immediate newborn period, does not prefer the father's voice to that of another male. Recognition of the father's voice comes slightly later. A newborn's preference for the mother's voice may be the enduring result of having heard it continually during fetal life. Infants also have a memory for stories or music they heard repeatedly in late fetal life.

Touch

The skin is the largest sense organ of the body. The sense of touch is activated early, since babies are surrounded and caressed by warm fluid and tissues from the beginning of fetal life. They like closeness, warmth, and tactile comforting. They generally like to be cuddled and will often nestle and mold to a parent's body. Parents all over the world naturally lift, hold, stroke, rock, and walk with their infants, as well as use other comforting touching motions to soothe their babies. Both parents and infants seem prepared to enjoy this experience.

Infants respond to the aspects of touch as well: variations in temperature, texture, moisture, pressure, and pain. The lips and hands have the most touch receptors; this may explain why newborns enjoy sucking their fingers. Ultrasound images show that fetuses suck their thumbs as early as twenty-four weeks. Touch is a major way that babies comfort themselves, explore their world, and initiate contact.

Taste

As with other sense organs, taste is also highly developed in infants at birth. Observations of what newborns choose to suck have shown that infants can make fine discriminations and are responsive to small chemical alterations in the foods placed on their tongues. Infants show pleasure as sweetness is increased and displeasure with slightly salty, acidic, or bitter liquids.[8]

Smell

Babies can distinguish among and recognize different smells. After initially responding to new smells, they quickly adapt and stop responding once the smell becomes familiar. When a novel smell is presented, they show interest by moving their heads; their activity level and heart rate change. By six days of life, each baby will even recognize the smell of his own mother.[9]

These incredible attributes of the newborn prepare the baby for interaction with the family and for life in the world.[10] Babies are born ready to gaze upon, cuddle close to, and listen to their parents, and to feed from their mothers.

4

BIRTH OF A FAMILY:

THE FIRST MINUTES

AND HOURS

"It's a girl!!" "It's a boy!!"
For new parents, those words bring an overwhelming surge of feeling, with tears of relief and joy. In these initial moments of bringing a baby into the world, something indescribably powerful happens for mothers and fathers that will remain etched in their minds forever. After the baby is dried and has adjusted to the outside world, and after the mother has finished the last stages of the delivery (the placenta has been delivered, any suturing has been done, and the mother has settled back in bed), the parents and the baby begin to get to know each other. With mother, father, and baby together, dramatic events are occurring in the baby, in the mother's body, and in the parents' minds and emotions. Our extensive exploration of these moments and the work of many other

investigators are gradually revealing some of what happens in the first hours.

An important clue to the mystery comes from observations of mothers and their recorded words when they first hold, touch, and begin to inspect their babies in privacy. Once they are left alone together, a mother usually focuses on her baby's eyes, as if to say, "Open your eyes, look at me." The baby also appears to have an interest in the parents. As we saw in the previous chapter, for the first forty-five minutes of life, most babies are in the quiet alert state, their eyes open in a bright, wide-eyed gaze when the light in the room is not too bright. Newborns seem especially prepared to greet their parents, and they are able to interact with their parents on many levels. Investigations using photographs have shown that the particular proportions of an infant's face—with a broad forehead, full, rounded cheeks, and shining, bright eyes—is particularly appealing to adults.

The extraordinary abilities of the newborn in this first alert period are suggested in the following brief examples from our experience. At a half hour of age, a baby girl was nestled in her mother's arms and was gazing at her mother's face. About fifteen minutes later the mother put on a pair of tortoise-shell glasses to look more closely at her baby. The baby then began to look at her mother's face with a very quizzical expression. She clearly was trying to integrate this new look of her mother. The mother recognized this change with surprise and delight and took off the glasses. Immediately the infant's face relaxed. We see here at least three remarkable talents in the newborn— the ability to see, to remember, and to note a change—in the first hour.

In another instance, a newborn boy and his mother and father had been having a very intense, quiet time while still in the delivery room looking at each other. The baby lay peacefully in his mother's arms. A nurse approached and said kindly, "Well, let me have Bobby for a minute now. I'm going to weigh him." When taken from his mother's arms, the baby immediately began to wail plaintively. Everybody was surprised because he had been so quiet. Another nurse suggested, "Why don't you put Bobby back in his mother's arms? He really seems to know the difference. Maybe you could measure him later." Back in his mother's arms, the baby quieted down again and settled very contentedly, again looking at his mother. Some-one commented, "He does seem to know the difference. Let's try that again." The same sequence was repeated, and again the baby wailed and then quieted again once he was with his mother. The doctor and nurses in the room agreed that he should be left in his mother's arms. "He really is giving us a message of where he is most happy. Let's not do this again," a nurse commented. This crying response on separation from the mother in the first minutes of life has been confirmed in a careful study.[1]

In a third family, a father who was an opera singer had been singing arias continually throughout his wife's pregnancy, arias for his baby-to-be. At the time of the birth he sang an aria—a piece that he had been rehearsing and singing in the preceding month—to welcome his baby into the world. As the baby came out into the world, she slowly turned her head to gaze in the direction of her father and listen continuously to his voice. No matter what happened through that first period right after birth, she kept looking at and listening to her father's voice with quiet attentiveness and interest. Near the end of the first hour of life when he sang again to her, her face turned to his and she responded with sounds, "Ah, ah, ah." Later, a short follow-up of this little girl showed that at three weeks of age in her crib, she appeared to be attempting to sing the scales as she listened to the rehearsal singing of her mother and father in the other room. Although studies have shown that babies recognize their mothers' voice shortly after birth, this has not been shown so early for fathers. To be sure, this was a special case, a baby who had had an unusual exposure to music.

These three examples suggest certain abilities in a newborn that cannot fail to engage the attention of new parents. When parents are cut off from such experience, the relationship has a very different start. A first-time mother who had not wanted anybody except her husband at the labor could not say no to several other family members who wanted to be present. Soon after the birth, which ended in an emergency cesarean section, everybody crowded around to inspect the baby, and the extended family over-whelmed the couple. Cynthia did not have the capacity to ask everybody to leave so that she could be alone with her baby and husband. When she finally had that first moment alone with her baby, it took place in the nursery where the baby had been taken. The mother experienced a very upsetting feeling of strangeness. She did not feel at all close to the baby, but instead felt confused and sad, as though the baby were somehow a stranger.

Through the whole first year of the baby's life, this mother worked hard at maintaining a good relationship with her and being a good mother, but Cynthia continued to feel very sad that this feeling of strangeness persisted. In talking about this event at length around the time of the baby's first birthday, she recognized that she was angry at the interference of these well-meaning family members and unknowingly displaced this repressed anger onto her baby. As she was able to express more of her anger in therapy, these feelings became resolved for her, and she began to see her baby in a very different light.

Reactions such as this one are usually seen in a milder form and are most often resolved by the parents in the first days of life. The presence of too many individuals during labor and delivery can be very disturbing to parents and can interrupt the natural psychological processes that take place. For years in our work we have tried to make caregivers on the obstetrical floor aware of how sensitive most fathers, mothers, and babies are. Interference during the process of labor and birth and distractions during the short early period afterward can have significant untoward effects.

WHEN DOES LOVE BEGIN?

Vital as these first moments are, they should not be expected to bring instant feelings of love for the infant. Since our first book on this subject appeared, a number of mothers have shared with us their distress and disappointment when they did not experience feelings of love for their baby in the first minutes or hours after birth. While we showed several variations, our work was interpreted to mean that instant bonding was universal.

Various investigators, also referred to in our earlier work, have put such a myth to rest. For instance, the British pediatrician Aidan MacFarlane and his associates asked ninety-seven Oxford mothers, "When did you first feel love for your baby?" The replies were as follows: during pregnancy, 41 percent; at birth, 24 percent; first week, 27 percent; and after the first week, 8 percent. Similar results were also recently observed.[2]

In two groups of first-time mothers studied at an earlier date, 40 percent recalled that their predominant emotional reaction when they first held their babies was one of indifference.[3] The same response was reported by 25 percent of forty mothers of more than one child. Forty percent of both groups felt immediate affection. Most of the mothers in both groups had developed affection for their babies within the first week. The onset of this maternal affection after childbirth was more likely to be delayed if the membranes had been ruptured artificially, if the labor had been long and painful, or if the mothers had received a generous dose of pain-killing medication. In many reports, the mother and father have noted that their loving and unique feelings for their baby began once they could have a private, quiet time together. Each parent takes on a new baby in a different fashion and at a different pace.

Recently, a woman who had extensive experience in caring for normal newborn infants told us about the birth of her first baby in a hospital where mothers and their infants stay together throughout the hospitalization. Following the birth, she checked her newborn over carefully and found him to be breathing easily and looking healthy, normal, and pink. She proceeded to feed and care for her baby, but she did not sense any passionate reaction to the newborn. Then, thirty-six hours after the birth when she was alone with the baby in the evening, she described a remarkable warm glow that came over her when she was looking at the baby's eyes. At that point she suddenly realized that she had the most perfect, most gorgeous, most responsive baby in the world. She experienced an incredible love for her infant.

How did this happen? What are the factors that result in either early or delayed feelings of love for a newborn infant? As an example of a different experience, a patient of one of the authors planned to take only two of her three allotted months of pregnancy leave because of her employment situation. Because she needed to return to work so soon after the birth, she felt conflict about whether she should begin breast-feeding. Her labor progressed slowly. She was given an epidural so that she could tolerate oxytocin augmentation. Her husband was anxious and very concerned when the baby's heart rate dropped briefly after the analgesia was started.

After the birth, this mother was exhausted, and her husband remained concerned about the baby even after the pediatrician said the baby was normal. At this particular hospital, the newborn baby is immediately placed in a warmer, where he or she is dried, measured, and briefly examined. The mother then took the baby for a short time, but she felt very tired and left the baby in the nursery, except for feedings.

Just before their discharge, the pediatrician discussed with her the benefits of breast-feeding, even if only for a month. She then mentioned her real concerns—her distress over getting too attached to the baby and then having to leave him to return to work full-time. In a slightly extended discussion with both parents, the pediatrician allowed the mother to explore her feelings and to cry over the dilemma about having to leave her baby. Her husband called the next day and described how much they both fell in love with this baby. And he explained that his wife had decided to breast-feed, despite the probable difficulties. She continued breast-feeding for six and a half months by using the breast pump at her office. Given time and reassurance, she was able to resolve her conflict and develop a deep and sustained bond to her child.

Emotional issues that do not get resolved or addressed during pregnancy will often reemerge when the baby is born. A complex script unfolds between parents and their infants, different for each set of parents, depending on their backgrounds, experiences, and current life situations.

Some fathers who are uninvolved during pregnancy have a welling up of emotion at the moment of birth. They have thoughts and feelings that surprise them as they experience an enormous love for their babies.

Sometimes after the birth, mothers who have felt perfectly prepared for the baby have memories or feelings activated or triggered about their own infancy, which may be different from what they had consciously thought of before the baby's birth. For example, one mother mentioned how unexpectedly sad she felt when she first explored her baby's face and looked into his eyes. A short time later she mentioned an impression of trying to get her mother to look at her. She recalled that she had been told that her mother had a clinical depression at the time of her birth and had not looked at her for some time. When this mother could separate her present situation from the experience she had had with her own mother, she could begin to enjoy her own baby.

Because there are many routes to becoming attached to one's baby, there is no reason for new mothers to be surprised and disappointed when they do not feel love immediately. Although the individual pace of a particular mother or father may require time, or unforeseen events may cause interferences, mothers and fathers can still have the exquisite sensation of falling in love with their babies.

The recommendations at the end of this chapter may help parents pave the way.

THE POWER OF EARLY CONTACT

As noted in earlier chapters, both mother and baby bring a wealth of inner resources to these early moments together. The single most important duty of caregivers at this time is to allow these natural abilities to blossom, and not to interfere.

Perhaps the most dramatic example of these astonishing natural talents is the ability of newborns, if left quietly on the mother's abdomen after birth, to crawl from the abdomen gradually up to her breast, find the nipple, and start to suckle. This difficult-to-believe ability has been described by Swedish investigators[4] and is shown in the photos in Illustration 4. If the mother has had no pain medicine during labor and her infant is dried and placed on her abdomen, kept warm with the heat of her body and a towel, and is not taken from the mother for the next seventy minutes, the baby usually begins a four-part sequence that ends with latching onto the mother's nipple. For the first thirty minutes, the newborn rests and looks up at the mother, on and off. At thirty to forty-five minutes, mouthing and lip-smacking movements begin, and the infant begins to drool. The baby then begins to inch forward, using his legs primarily. When he reaches the level of the mother's nipple, he begins to turn his head vigorously from side to side, open-ing his mouth widely. After several tries he generally latches onto the areola, the brown portion around the nipple (see also Chapter 5). The odor of the nipple appears to guide the newborn to the breast. If the right breast is washed with soap and water, the infant will crawl to the left breast, and vice versa.[5]

In the group of mothers studied who did not receive pain medication and whose babies were not taken away during the first hours of life for baths, vitamin K, or eye ointment, fifteen out of sixteen babies were observed to make this trip all on their own and to begin to suckle effectively.[6] These and other observations have made us question our present policy of put-ting infants to the breast, immediately after birth. In this newly discovered process, it appears that the newborn begins suckling at a more appropriate time, after recovering from the stress of birth. At this point, the infant is probably more ready to begin to eat. Raven Lang, a mid-wife, observed in a study of home births that when offered the breast, the baby often does not suck at first. Rather, the most common action for the baby when first given the mother's nipple is to lick it.[7]

Certain Swedish investigators also have noted that if the lips of the infant touch the nipple in the first hour of life, a mother will decide to keep her baby longer in her own room during her hospital stay than another mother who did not have contact until later.[8] Multiple studies have shown that if the infant suckles in the first hour of life, the mother and infant will be much more successful at breast-feeding, making it more likely that the mother will choose to breast-feed for several months. Other Swedish researchers have shown that the normal infant, when dried and placed nude on the mother's chest and then covered with a blanket, will maintain his or her body temperature as well or better than in the elaborate, high-tech heating devices that usually separate the mother and baby.[9] The same researchers found that when the infants are skin-to-skin with their mothers, for the first ninety minutes, they cry hardly at all, compared to infants who were wrapped in a towel and placed in a bassinet. It seems likely that each of these features—the crawling ability of the infant, the sensitivity of the mother's nipple, and the warming capabilities of the mother's chest—are adaptive and were built into human beings millions of years ago, during much more stressful times, to help preserve the infant's life.

Another characteristic pattern in the first hours after birth, described by several observers, is a kind of gentle, at first tentative, touching. Reva Rubin, a pioneer nurse researcher, observed mothers and their new infants over a three-day period and noted that mothers show an orderly progression of behavior while becoming acquainted with their babies.[10] In another study done by the authors and colleagues, nude infants were placed next to their mothers at a few minutes or one hour after birth, and left alone. The mothers tended to touch them in a pattern of behavior that began with fingertip touching of the infant's arms and legs and proceeded in seven to eight minutes to gentle massaging, stroking, and encompassing whole-hand contact on the body and head.[11] In those first three minutes, the mothers maintained fingertip contact 52 percent of the time and palm contact 28 percent of the time. In the last three minutes of observation (after seven to ten minutes), however, this was reversed. Fingertip contact greatly decreased, and palm contact increased to 62 percent of the total time.

In her study of home births mentioned earlier, Lang observed that the mother almost always rubs the baby's skin, starting with the face. Rubbing is done with the fingertips and is usually a gentle stroking motion. This occurs before delivery of the placenta and before the initial breast-feeding.

In more recent studies, somewhat different approaches taken by mothers as they first touch their babies have been found.[12,13] Differences in factors such as the study environments, the amount of time the mothers and babies were separated following birth, and the mothers' cultural backgrounds might account for the variations noted in the studies.

An observation by Swedish researchers offers additional insights about the meaning of the sequence of touching behaviors.[14] They observed that unrelated adults (medical students) have a touching sequence with a young infant much like that of parents. Is this sequence the natural process by which humans approach an infant? Is it built into our biology? Or is it simply the way most adults have learned to approach small creatures?

A mother's or father's behavior toward an infant results from a complex combination of the infant's responses to the parent, the parent's own genetic endowments, a long history of interpersonal relationships inside and outside the family, experiences with this or previous pregnancies, the absorption of the practices and values of the broader culture, and the way each parent was raised by his or her own parents. Other factors—such as the attitudes, statements, and practices of the nurses and physicians in the hospital; whether the mother is alone for short periods during her labor; any separation of the mother from the infant in the first days of life; the infant's temperament and overall health—will obviously all affect parenting behavior. The impact of some of these early-life experiences on parental attitudes and behavior may be changed or affected both favorably and unfavorably during the crisis of birth and the first few days afterward.

Winnicott's observations on this time period are useful to review:[15]

> I cannot find words to express what big forces are at work at this critical point, but I can try to explain something of what is going on. There is a most curious thing happening: the mother who is perhaps physically exhausted, and perhaps incontinent, and who is dependent on the nurse and the doctor for skilled attention in many and various ways, is at the same time the one person who can properly introduce the world to the baby in a way that makes sense to the baby. She knows how to do this, not through any training and not through being clever, but just because she is the natural mother. Her natural instincts cannot evolve if she is scared, or if she does not see her baby when it is born, or if the baby is brought to her only at stated times thought by the authorities to be suitable for feeding purposes. It just does not work that way.

The intense power of early contact to shape a mother's

attachment to her baby is illustrated in the following two unusual episodes from the authors' experience—one in Israel and the other in Argentina.

In an Israeli hospital mix-up, two mothers were inadvertently given, and consequently took home and cared for, the wrong babies. At the two-week infant checkup, the error was discovered and efforts were made to return the babies to their own families. However, each mother had become so attached to the baby she had cared for during the first fourteen days that she was reluctant to give the baby up. The husbands, on the other hand, strongly supported correcting the error because of facial and other characteristics unique to the individual families.

In Buenos Aires, Argentina, a similar mistaken switch of babies occurred, but was discovered while the mothers were still in the hospital. The two families were so angry that they refused to talk or cooperate with the hospital personnel. A wise neonatologist proposed that the two mothers be placed overnight in the same room with the two babies. For the first several hours, each mother remained silent while holding the baby she had been given originally. Finally, one mother said, "We will be together here for another twenty hours. Let us at least talk." As she was saying these words, she noticed that the baby held by the other mother turned toward her, and at that moment she recognized the appearance of her own mother in the baby's face. She then realized that each time one mother talked, the other baby would respond. It became clear to each mother that something about her voice was familiar to the baby held by the other mother. Each mother began to see family characteristics in the baby that had originally been assigned to the other mother. Each then happily accepted her biological baby.

Over the years, studies of the effects of rooming-in—of having a mother and baby stay together in a room after the birth—have also confirmed the importance of contact during the early postnatal period. An increase in breast-feeding and a reduction in anxious phone calls to the doctor after returning home were noted after rooming-in was instituted a number of years ago at Duke University.[16] In Sweden, mothers randomly assigned to rooming-in arrangements were more confident, felt more competent in caregiving, and appeared more sensitive to the cries of their own infants than mothers who did not have rooming-in.[17] More recently, in Thailand, in a hospital where a disturbing number of babies were abandoned by their mothers, the use of rooming-in and early contact significantly reduced the frequency of this sad outcome, from 33 abandoned babies to 1 per year.[18] Similar observations on a striking decrease in abandonment of infants in maternity hospitals have also been made in the Philippines and Costa Rica when early contact with breast-feeding and rooming-in were introduced (in the Philippines it was part of the Baby Friendly Initiative).[19]

All these reports suggest that the events occurring in the first hours and days after birth have special significance for the mother. Speaking to mothers, Winnicott noted another reason why early contact is important:[20]

> I think an important thing about a young mother's experience of early contact with her baby is the reassurance that it gives her that her baby is normal. . . . You may be too exhausted to start making friends with your baby on the first day, but it is well that you should know that it is entirely natural that a mother should want to get to know her baby right away after birth. This is not only because she longs to know him [or her], it is also—and it is this that makes it an urgent matter—because she has had all sorts of ideas of giving birth to something awful, something certainly not so perfect as a baby. It is as if human beings find it very difficult to believe that they are good enough to create within themselves something that is quite good. I doubt whether any mother really and fully believes in her child at the begin-

ning. Father comes into this too, for he suffers just as much as mother does from the doubt that he may not be able to create a normal, healthy child. Getting to know your baby is therefore in the first place an urgent matter because of the relief that the good news brings to both parents.

His sensitive observations may explain in part why mothers who gave birth years earlier and who were separated from their babies at birth because of hospital practices of the time will often repress those memories until sometime later when they are talking to others about their childbirth experiences. When learning about the new choices women have today to be more in charge of the birth experience—for example, creating birth plans, choosing early suckling, rooming-in—they will often feel sad as they remember those hours or days of separation.

A SENSITIVE PERIOD?

Probably no perinatal caregiving practice in hospitals has been studied more intensively than the timing of the moment when a mother is to receive her baby after birth. Researchers have focused on the question of whether there is a sensitive period for parent–infant contact in the first minutes, hours, or days of life that may alter the parents' later behavior with that infant. In many biological disciplines these moments have been called sensitive periods, vulnerable periods, or susceptible periods.

In the 1930s and 1940s, a mother typically did not receive her baby for several hours after giving birth, because she was asleep from drugs. This early separation practice continued well into the 1970s and 1980s. Many women came to believe that this separation was "normal" because of the prevailing medical practices of the time. But many actually felt lonely for their babies and yet were intimidated or confused about what was appropriate.

In the early studies exploring a sensitive period, investigators focused on whether increasing the opportunity for close contact between the mother and her full-term infant in the first minutes, hours, and days of life alters the quality of the mother–infant interaction over time. It is important to remember that when the first study of early contact was undertaken, mothers who had a typical hospital birth stayed five or more days in the hospital and there was no rooming-in. A mother first saw her baby for a brief identification at six to twelve hours after birth. Then the babies were kept in the central nursery and brought out to their mothers only every four hours for a twenty-minute feeding.

Detailed observations in these first studies revealed significantly more maternal affectionate behavior in the first days and early weeks of life when mothers had additional time for early and extended contact with their full-term infants in the hospital. As an example, in the first study that provided early mother–infant contact, the group of poor, primarily single, inner-city mothers of first babies were given sixteen hours of extra contact with their infants in the first three days of life.[21] Subsequently, at one month this group of mothers fed their infants with more affectionate attention and they gave more comforting, attentive, loving responses when their infants cried during stressful office visits, than did a control group of mothers who had received their infants later and then had had them only for twenty-minute feedings every four hours.

One of the strongest findings was related to breast-feeding. Seven of nine studies revealed that when a mother wanted to breast-feed and was permitted to have early contact with her infant, with an opportunity for suckling in the first hour of life, she was far more successful than mothers who did not have such experiences. She succeeded in initiating breast-feeding and was able to breast-feed for a longer period than mothers who did not have early contact and suckling with their babies. Consequently, this became one of ten caregiving procedures UNICEF developed as part of its Baby Friendly Initiative to increase breast-feeding throughout the world.

Of potentially even greater significance were the later observations by pediatrician Susan O'Connor and her team of investigators. She provided twelve additional hours of mother–infant
contact in the first two days of life for one group of 134 women in
a population with a high incidence of social problems compared to
a similar control group of 143 women who received the typical
limited amount of contact.[22] Contact in the first hour was not
offered to either group of mothers. During the first seventeen
months of the babies' lives, significantly more parenting disorders
arose among the group who had not had additional contact (ten
versus two). These disorders included child abuse, abandonment,
and neglect.

In a similar study in North Carolina involving 202 mothers,
researchers did not find a statistically significant difference in the
frequency of parenting disorders: ten children were abused or
neglected or failed to thrive in the control group (105 mothers)
versus seven in the extended-contact group (97 mothers).[23] They
did, however, find differences in how the mothers reacted to their
infants at four and twelve months. In addition to increasing early
contact, investigators tried showing mothers some of their newborns' abilities (to follow the mother's face, to turn to her voice,
and so on) and helping the mothers discover what actions would
quiet their infants. These mothers became more interactive with
their babies face-to-face and during feedings at three and four
months of age.[24]

Further confirmation of the effect of extended early contact
on maternal behavior was found in a study done with sixty
mothers and their newborns in Portugal.[25] Increased affectionate
and soothing behavior four weeks after birth were shown by the
mothers who were given their babies for a period alone together
immediately after birth. Although debate on the interpretation and
significance of the many research studies continues regarding the
effects that early and extended contact for mothers and fathers has

on parents' ability to bond with their infants, all sides agree that all parents should be offered such contact time with their infants. In a recent extensive review of this subject, researchers reached the following conclusions: [26]

> We have been unable to find any evidence suggesting that the restriction of early postnatal mother–infant interaction which has been such a common feature of the care of women giving birth in hospitals has any beneficial effects. On the contrary, the available evidence suggests that any effects that these restrictive policies have are undesirable. The data suggest the plausible hypothesis that women of low socioeconomic status may be particularly vulnerable to the adverse effects of restricting contact.

> It may be thought surprising that disruption of maternal–infant interaction in the immediate postnatal period may set some women on the road to breast-feeding failure and altered subsequent behaviour towards their children. Paediatricians, psychologists, and others have indeed debated this issue. This skepticism does not, however, constitute grounds for acquiescing in hospital routines which lead to unwanted separation of mothers from their babies. In the light of the evidence that such policies may actually do harm, they should be changed forthwith.

Clinically, what does seem apparent from the research and the authors' experience is that in a large number of maternity units, a mother who receives routine care involving total separation from her child after a glimpse at birth may not feel confident that the baby is healthy or even breathing. She may not experience the flood of positive feelings that the beauty and responsiveness of her baby could have released; she may feel lonely, empty, deprived, and worried that the baby has some problem. In addition, the study of doula support during labor described in Chapter 2 indicates that mothers who have had supportive companions during labor have a greater interest in interacting with their babies in the first hour after birth. This can trigger feelings of enhanced self-esteem and accomplishment and a series of interactions with the baby—part of the chain reaction that contributes to the formation of a strong and enduring bond.

In summary, increasing evidence from many studies has pointed to a sensitive period that is significant to the bonding experience. However, as we have already stated, this does not imply that all mothers and fathers develop a close tie to their infants within a few minutes of the first contact. Because of the multiple environmental influences that occur during this period, each parent does not react in a standard or predictable fashion. Individual differences in mothers and fathers also influence their reactions. Nevertheless, when we enable parents to be together in privacy with their baby for the first hour and throughout the hospital stay, and add supportive caregiving, we establish the environment most conducive to the beginning of the bonding process.

FATHERS

Fathers become attached to their new infants in their own ways. Although changes in our society and the expectations of young parents have sometimes implied that the roles of father and mother may be in some ways interchangeable, we tend to agree with Winnicott that, for many tasks, each parent has a separate and distinct role. A father is not merely a replacement for a mother, but a primary nurturer for his newborn.

The pediatrician and researcher Michael Yogman noted that the time prior to the birth of a baby is a time requiring psychological readjustment for both parents as they integrate the roles of child and spouse with that of expectant parent.[27] However, the expectant father does not feel the physical presence of the fetus growing within him, and this may stimulate a father to search for alternative evidence of his productivity and creativity, especially through increased attention to his work and the provision of financial security for his family. The struggle for the expectant male during the prenatal period is to remain emotionally available to his wife, while also trying to feel responsible and productive. Many observers have noted that when the husband is responsive and caring to his wife during pregnancy, she more successfully adapts to the pregnancy.

The term *engrossment* (meaning "absorption, preoccupation, and interest") has been used to describe the powerful response fathers often feel toward their newborn.[28] Engrossment includes several specific aspects of the father's developing bond to his newborn, ranging from his attraction to the infant, to his perception of the newborn as "perfect," to extreme elation and an increased sense of self-esteem.

Through careful observations, the psychologist Ross Parke showed that fathers are just as responsive as mothers to infant cues such as vocalizations.[29] Both fathers and mothers increase their rate of cooing and responding following a sound from the infant. However, fathers and mothers differ in the behavior they show in response to an infant's vocalization. Fathers are more likely to talk rapidly, whereas mothers are more likely to respond with touching. Parke notes that "the data indicate that fathers and mothers both react to the newborn infant's cues in a contingent and functional manner even though they differ in their specific response patterns." (He noted that fathers and mothers are not only similar in their sensitivity to the infant but are equally successful in bottle-feeding the infant based on the amount of milk consumed.) Newborns themselves contribute to a father's attachment and involvement. The infant psychiatrist Daniel Stern notes that infants respond to, and are in tune in a selective manner with each parent and can recognize and respond to the father's voice patterns.[30]

Parke believes that the father must have an extensive early exposure to the infant in the hospital, where the parent–infant bond is initially formed. "There is a lot of learning that goes on between the mother and infant in the hospital—from which the father is excluded and in which he must be included so he'll not only have the interest and a feeling of owning the baby, but also the kinds of skills that the mother develops." Parke concluded that the father is much more interested in, and responsive toward, his infant than U.S. culture has fully acknowledged. Other researchers [31] have found that paternal caregiving in an infant's first three months of life is greatly increased when a father is asked to undress and dress his infant twice and to establish eye-to-eye contact with the infant for an hour during the first three days of life.

Different hospital policies following cesarean birth in two maternity hospitals in Goteborg, Sweden, made it possible to study the effect of allowing fathers to handle their newborn infants immediately after birth. [32] One group of fathers who were allowed this early contact was compared with another group whose infants were kept in incubators and who were permitted only to look at them. In a play situation three months later, the early-contact fathers touched their infants more and more often held them with the baby's face toward them than did the noncontact fathers. The barrier of the incubator may have had a contributory effect, but these differences suggest that early contact might have altered paternal behavior. Similar findings have been noted in the United States. T. Berry Brazelton compared fathers who had different experiences with first and second babies. "The fathers I have worked with have told me that their own excitement in being included in labor and birth not only attaches them to the baby differently from the first baby, but it gives them a very different feeling of closeness to their wives—having shared such an intimate, important event. [33]

In the situations when a mother cannot be with her infant immediately after the birth, the infant can receive the necessary warmth and security from the father while the mother recovers. One six-year-old boy surprised his mother one day by saying,

"Mommie, when I was born, I was in a box. You weren't there, but it was okay because Daddy stayed with me." The mother reported this with astonishment, and it was true. The boy had been born three weeks early, and his mother had had an emergency cesarean section with general anesthesia. Her recovery had been slow, and she had not been able to see or hold her baby for twenty-four hours. She had always felt bad about this delay and had secretly believed that she had deprived her son of her presence, so she had not talked about the experience. His comment reassured her.

Another mother with whom we spoke felt deeply sad that she had not been able to hold her baby immediately after her cesarean. In reviewing the birth, she recognized that her husband had had the baby in his arms within a minute after the delivery and that the baby had looked contently at him. Also, she learned that she had been under anesthesia for a much shorter time than she had thought. Once she became aware of this, she experienced a surge of love for the baby and an inner security in knowing the feelings that her husband had for her and the baby.

THE FIRST HOURS TOGETHER

As the mother and baby rest together after birth, a cascade of sensory, hormonal, physiological, immunological, and behavioral events begin to occur. Several of these probably contribute to the mother's attachment to her infant, gradually locking them together and ensuring the further development of their relationship.

An important first step in understanding this period was the identification of six separate states of consciousness in the infant, ranging from deep sleep to crying (see Chapter 3).[34] The state with which we are most concerned is the quiet alert state. In this state the infant's eyes are wide open, and she is able to respond to her environment. Infants remain in this quiet alert state for an average of forty-three minutes during the first hour after birth. In this state, the infant's broad array of sensory and motor abilities evokes responses from the mother and father and opens several channels of communication with them. The parents are intensely interested in looking into the newborn's open eyes. A special intimacy often begins in the first hours of life (Illustration 5). When alert, the newborn is visually able to follow the parent's face over an arc of 180 degrees.

The fascinating question of how parental attachment progresses during the early postpartum period can be answered only by minutely examining what happens between parents and their newborn during this crucial time. What pulls them together, ensuring their proximity through the many months during which the infant is unable to satisfy his own needs? What are the rewards for the mother's commitment and efforts? Take the picture of a common situation—a mother feeding her infant in the first hour of life. The simplicity of this scene obscures the multiple interactions simultaneously occurring between mother and child. Each is intimately involved with the other on a number of levels, which lock the pair together. The mother and baby elicit behaviors in each other that are naturally rewarding. For example, the infant's crying is likely to bring the mother near and trigger her to pick him up. When she picks him up, he is likely to quiet, open his eyes, and follow her movements. When the mother starts the communication by touching the infant's cheek, he is likely to turn his head, bringing him into contact with her nipple, on which he will suck. His sucking in turn is pleasurable to both of them. This is a necessarily oversimplified description of these interactions; the behaviors do not occur in a chainlike sequence, but rather each event triggers several others. When we look closely, we see a fail-safe system that ensures the proximity of mother and child.

Because of the limitations of language, the interactions must be described sequentially rather than simultaneously, sacrificing the richness of the actual process for the sake of understanding them.

Eye-to-Eye Contact

One interaction that proceeds back and forth from mother to child originates in the eyes. We have observed that mothers who are alone with their infants shortly after birth show a strong interest in eye-to-eye contact. Seventy-three percent of the mothers in a group we studied described an intense interest in waking their infants to see the eyes open. Some expressed a feeling that the baby's eyes showed aliveness or love, and several mentioned that once the infant looked at them, they felt much closer to her. The mothers and fathers showed a remarkable increase (from ten percent of the time to twenty-three percent of the time) in the time spent in the *en face* position (parent and infant face-to-face, with their heads aligned in the same parallel plane) from the first to the fifth minute.[35]

Raven Lang observed that in most home births immediately after the birth of the baby, but before the delivery of the placenta, the mother picked up the baby and held him in the en face position while speaking to him in a high-pitched voice.[36] In the photo on page 75, a mother of a full-term infant is shown en face while the father observes the infant. Other factors foster this rewarding eye-to-eye contact:

> The appeal of the mother's eyes to the child (and of his eyes to her) is facilitated by their richness. In comparison with other areas of the body, the eye has a remarkable array of interesting qualities such as the shininess of the globe, the fact that it is mobile while at the same time fixed in space, the contrasts between the pupil-iris-cornea configuration, and the capacity of the pupil to vary in diameter.[37]

The psychoanalyst Selma Fraiberg has described in detail the difficulties that parents of blind infants have in feeling close to them.[38] Without the affirmation of mutual gazing, parents feel lost and like strangers to their babies until both learn to substitute other means of communication.

While performing the Brazelton Neonatal Behavior Assessment on large numbers of infants, we have been repeatedly struck by how often the babies have preferred looking at the examiner's face rather than inanimate objects. Others have established that one of the earliest and most effective stimuli for eliciting a social smile in an infant is a visual configuration consisting of two eyes and a mouth shown en face. This is the innate form preference of newborns, minutes after birth, even before there has been any opportunity for the infant to see human faces.[39] Parents tend to look at their babies in a way that increases the chance that their babies will attend and follow and then, a bit later, smile back. Since smiling is an extremely powerful reinforcer, this visual interaction is important in bringing about the closeness of parent and child.

The power of eye-to-eye contact with a newborn has been brought home to us repeatedly. For example, three young researchers who were participating in a separate study with us were required to assist with Brazelton Neonatal Behavior Assessments on infants each day. We were distressed to hear all three say that they did not particularly like babies, found newborns especially unappealing, and planned never to have a baby. They grumbled about having to learn the behavioral assessments. As they carried out the assessments, each of the women had her first experience with a baby in the alert state, following her eyes with his own. An amazing change occurred. Suddenly each became enthusiastic about "her" baby, wanted to hold him, and came back later in the day and the next day to visit. In the evening, she would tell her friends about this marvelous baby she had tested. In a few weeks all three had decided they would someday like to have a baby. The experience of these three women is common and demonstrates the compelling attraction of a newborn infant moving her eyes to follow an adult's eyes, and the layer upon layer of emotional meaning that the viewer may place on this.

Mother's Voice and Baby's Cry

Parents and babies both respond to vocal cues. Newborns can discriminate between a woman's and a man's voice, and even between two women's voices if one is their mother's, as we discussed in Chapter 3. They show a preference for the mother's voice. Soon after birth some babies demonstrate that they recognize a story that had been read and repeated to them while in the uterus. As noted in Chapter 3, parents and others are drawn to speak to infants in a high-pitched voice, and newborns become alert and respond to high-pitched voices, showing their preference for speech in the high-frequency range. In addition to the mother's voice affecting the infant's response, the infant's cry elicits a physiological change in the mother that is likely to induce her to nurse. After being exposed to the hunger cries of healthy newborns, 90 percent of a large group of mothers demonstrated a significant increase in the amount of blood flow to their breasts, as shown by thermal photography.[40] This showed that mothers respond at a physiologic level to the infant's sounds. Within this wonderfully complex, interactive system, a mother can identify her own infant's voice a day or two after birth, but not as quickly as the infant can.[41]

Entrainment

When sound films are analyzed second by second, we see that human communication involves not only sound but movement. When a person speaks, several parts of his body move in ways that are sometimes obvious, sometimes almost imperceptible; the same is true of the listener, whose movements are coordinated to the elements of the speech. This "microanalysis" of films reveals that both the listener and the speaker are moving in tune to the speaker's words, thus creating a type of dance. The rhythm of the dance is the pattern of the speech. This interaction is called *entrainment* and cannot be seen with the naked eye, but the players pick it up at a subliminal level.

We can speculate that before birth, many of the fetus's actions and rhythms are attuned to those of the mother. This is caused by a variety of rhythmical influences—the sleep-wake cycles of the mother, the daily fluctuations of her hormones, the orderly patterns of her day, the regular beat of her heart, and the rhythmic contractions of the uterus preceding the onset of labor and continuing up to the time that the baby emerges from the birth canal. These prenatal influences probably increase the likelihood of the newborn's response to the presence, voice, and actions of the mother.

Newborns move in rhythm to the structure of adult speech. "When the infant is already in movement, points of change in the configuration of his moving body parts become coordinated with points of change in sound patterns characterizing speech."[42] As the adult speaker pauses for breath or accents a syllable, the infant almost imperceptibly raises an eyebrow or lowers a foot. Actual, live speech in particular is most effective in entraining infant movement. Neither tapping noises nor disconnected vowel sounds show the degree of correspondence with the newborn's motions as do natural, rhythmical speech patterns. To date, in all languages studied, synchronous movement has been observed.

> If the infant, from the beginning, moves in precise, shared rhythm with the organization of the speech structure of his culture, then he participates developmentally through complex, socio-biological entrainment processes in millions of repetitions of linguistic forms long before he later uses them in speaking and communicating.[43]

While the infant moves in rhythm to his mother's voice and thus may be said to be affected by her, his movements may, in turn, reward the mother and stimulate her to continue. Their dialogue is thus interactive and self-sustaining.

From numerous clinical experiences, we believe that during their first encounters, parents usually receive some response or signal, such as body or eye movements, from their infant. We believe that for most parents this vital acknowledgment takes place in the first days of life, when the infant is in the quiet alert state and moves in rhythm to the parents' speech.

The psychiatrist and researcher Louis Sander has identified a progressive increase in the infant's being in a quiet alert state in response to being held by her mother.[44] This increases from less than 25 percent on the second day to 57 percent on the eighth day, a finding that led him to compare the mother's effect on the infant to the effect of a magnet in organizing and lining up iron filings.

Sander has emphasized that the quiet alert state in a young infant is extremely stable. He has shown that if the baby is in any other state and the mother or father intervenes, the baby will then probably move into the quiet alert state. However, babies' responses are often motivated by how they are feeling emotionally, and sometimes they may not do this. If the baby is already in the quiet alert state and the mother intervenes, there is only a slight chance of change in state. The high occurrence of the alert state results from the interaction of a sensitive mother (or other caregiver) with her infant.

Hormone Levels

As we mentioned, the infant can also initiate the secretion of the maternal hormones oxytocin and prolactin. Breast-feeding the infant or having him lick the mother's nipple leads to the release of oxytocin (i.e., the let-down reflex) by the mother, which hastens uterine contractions and reduces bleeding. After breast-feeding is under way, the sight or a reminder of the infant results in the let-down reflex. Each suckling period increases the oxytocin level, which has a calming effect on the mother and also tends to increase the tie the mother has to her infant. The latter effect is the reason oxytocin has been called the "cuddle hormone."[45]

In addition, when the infant suckles from the breast, there is a large outpouring of twenty different gastrointestinal hormones in both the mother and the infant, including cholocystokinins, which stimulate the growth of the baby's intestines and increase the absorption of calories with each feeding. The stimuli for this release are carried by the mother's nipple and the inside of the infant's mouth. These responses were essential for survival thousands of years ago when periods of famine were more common before the development of modern agriculture.[46] Also, whenever the nipple of the mother is touched, either by the infant's lips or by a finger, there is a fourfold to sixfold increase in her prolactin level. After breast-feeding begins, the level decreases. These changes in prolactin levels induce the alveoli of the breasts to produce milk.

Women who, through nipple stimulation by the baby, have been able to breast-feed their adopted babies have also reported the rapid development of strong feelings of closeness and attachment while breast-feeding. In these situations skin-to-skin contact, touch, smell, body warmth, and auditory and visual stimuli, as well as maternal hormones, probably all operate together to promote attachment.

Smell and Touch

Both mothers and babies can find each other through the sense of smell, as we noted in Chapter 3. A mother can pick out her infant among other infants through smell within the first day after birth, after having had only one hour of contact.[47] A baby, on the other hand, takes about six days to distinguish the odor of her mother's breast pads from the odor of other mothers' breast pads.

Touch and smell are the first and most basic means by which a mother identifies her infant.[48] In one study, twenty-four hours after birth, mothers who had had more than one hour with their infants and who were then blindfolded and had their other senses (e.g., smell, hearing) blocked could identify their own infants from two other infants by touching the backs of the babies' hands.

It is curious that a mother recognizes her infant's odor and the feel of the baby's skin earlier than she remembers the sound of the baby's cry or a photo of the baby. The mother is sensing the baby at many different levels. The whole system appears to enable the mother to communicate with her infant in ways that can bypass the logical and rational areas of the brain and allow the mother to take in and sense the baby at a deeper, more primitive level.

Imitation

When quiet and alert, babies will often gaze at their parents' faces with special interest and pleasure, and they can not only respond to what they see but also imitate some of what they see in their parents' faces.[49] If a newborn is looking directly at his mother's face and the mother sticks out her tongue, the newborn will, after about thirty to forty-five seconds, tense his body slightly and begin to push his tongue out.

How do babies accomplish such a remarkable feat? They must somehow sense that they have a tongue, as well as where it is located and how to control it. The act of imitation is a complex affair. It is wonderful to realize that a newborn—never having looked in a mirror, never having played the toddler game of finding her own nose or her mother's nose—somehow recognizes that what she is seeing in her mother's face relates to a part of her own body.

This game can affect the behavior of both mother and baby in strange ways. One mother described how her baby yawned, which inspired her to yawn. The baby yawned again, and the process continued until they both fell asleep. Winnicott observed that mothers are mirrors for their babies and spend much time in the first months of life imitating their infants. He commented, "What does the baby see when he or she looks at the mother's face? I am suggesting that, ordinarily, what the baby sees is himself or herself."[50] Thus, the mother and the infant imitate each other.

These back-and-forth responses become especially important as the infant is beginning to discover her own being or
boundaries. Babies appear to become more responsive when
mothers gently follow or imitate them rather than stimulate or
lead them. Imitation of the infant's actions aids the process of self-
discovery. This mutual mirroring is yet another way that infants
learn about themselves, their parents, and the ways to act in their
society. It is not a deliberate, self-conscious activity, but a natural
process that takes place unconsciously.

As parents spend time getting to know their baby, they gradually learn to put themselves in their infant's place. When they do, the
signals the baby sends out make her needs known and elicit an
appropriate response from the parents. Thus, within us all are
powerful inborn systems for communicating, nurturing, and surviving.

In this initial period, if mothers have fears about their babies'
health or their own well-being, or if they do not feel supported by
their partners, these concerns may affect how they feel toward
their new babies. In addition, some mothers feel disappointed and
very sad when, because of surgery or illness at birth, they cannot
hold their babies immediately. They wonder and worry that they
or their babies have missed something crucial. Parents need to be
reassured that not holding the baby in the first hours of life is not
a tragedy, that all is not lost, and that there are many times in the
ensuing days and weeks in which the bond of love grows. It
appears that there are numerous built-in human systems that tie
the mother and father to their baby so that the development of the
relationship seems almost fail-safe.

CONCLUSION

In reporting on our years of research into parent–infant
bonding, we have faced a real dilemma in deciding how strongly to

emphasize the importance of contact in the first hour and extended visiting for the rest of the hospital stay. Obviously, even parents who have lacked early contact with their infants after hospital births generally become bonded to their babies. Human beings are highly adaptable, and many routes to attachment unfold. Sadly, some parents who missed the early bonding experience have thought that all was lost for their future relationship with their child. This belief was (and is) completely incorrect, but it was so upsetting to such parents that we have tried to speak more cautiously about our convictions concerning the long-term significance of this early bonding experience. Unfortunately, we find that doing so has led some skeptics to discontinue the practice of early contact, to emphasize routine treatments in an electronic warmer in the first hour, or to make a slapdash, rushed charade of the parent–infant contact. In these situations, there is a lack of attention to the privacy, support, and patience necessary for early and extended contact. The mothers who miss out are often those at the limits of adaptability and who stand to benefit the most—the poor, the single, the unsupported, and the teenage mothers.

We believe that there is firm evidence for the benefits of early contact between parents and infants immediately after birth. Less than an hour alone together in private is almost certainly inadequate. While studies have not clarified how much of the effect may be apportioned to the first hours and how much to the first days, additional contact in both periods helps mothers and fathers become acquainted with their babies. For some mothers, one period may be more important than the other.

If the health of the mother or infant makes this early contact impossible, then discussion, support, and reassurance should help the parents appreciate that they can become as completely attached to their infant as if they had had the usual bonding experience, although the process may require more time. Obviously, the infant should be with the parents only if she is known to be physically normal, and if appropriate temperature control is maintained. We also strongly urge that the infant remain with the mother as long as the mother wishes throughout the (now very short) hospital stay so that she and the baby can get to know each other. Happily, placement in a large central nursery is being phased out for most babies. Allowing the infant to be with the mother offers more opportunity for both mother and father to learn about their baby, to ask questions at a time when caregivers are still available, and to begin to develop a bond in the first weeks of their baby's life.

RECOMMENDATIONS

To put into practice what is known about the importance of this period for parents and their baby, along with the reality of the economic pressures and time constraints that have reduced the hospital stay to twelve to thirty-six hours, we make the following recommendations. Parents would do well to discuss them with their doctor or hospital personnel before birth.

1. *The first hour.* After the baby has been well dried, the placenta has been delivered, and any suturing has been completed (usually five to fifteen minutes after the actual delivery), the parents should have a period of at least one hour alone together in privacy with their baby.

2. *Privacy.* This period must be arranged as a private time for parents and their baby. Falling in love with one's baby cannot occur in the middle of a bustling room full of people.

3. *Rooming-in.* If at all possible, unless there is a true medical indication, babies should not be separated from their parents throughout the hospital stay.

4. *Warmth.* Right after birth, the baby should be dried thoroughly, and a triple-layered hat should be put on. Once the baby is pink and active (greater than 90 percent of babies reach this state within a few minutes after delivery), the baby should be allowed to be with the parents in a comfortable fashion that ensures the baby's continued warmth. The infant will maintain the proper temperature if placed skin-to-skin with the mother and covered by a warm, dry towel or a light blanket, or next to the mother with a heat panel or warmer over both of them.

5. *Letting the baby find the breast.* If the mother plans to breast-feed, even for a short time, the parents should be asked if they would like to allow the baby to maneuver up to the breast and begin to breast-feed on its own (see pages 62 and 63). To allow this to occur, the baby should not be taken away from the mother during the first hour of life. Measuring the infant, administering vitamin K and eye ointment, and bathing the infant must be saved for later.

6. *Early responsibility.* Healthy parents should be given complete responsibility for the care of their infant, with nurses or midwives available as consultants when the parents wish to have help. Reversing the usual pattern of the "expert" who corrects the mother when she deviates from the usual routine is a step in the direction of increased confidence for the mother.

7. *Incubators and light treatment.* We suggest that, when possible, infants requiring additional heat remain in an incubator next to the mother. This would include babies who are slightly small for gestational age. For babies with jaundice, we recommend that bilirubin light treatments take place in the mother's room.

8. *Timing of advice.* All instructions should be paced and adapted to the individual needs of each woman and her baby. As an example, if a mother is finding it difficult to have the baby latch onto the breast, it will be hard for her to listen to any routine instructions—about such things as bathing, care of the navel and the skin, and the need for routine screening tests—until she has completed that task. Instructions should be geared to the educational level of the mother and presented in an interesting manner.

9. *New mothers groups.* Discussions of common issues about personal care and the baby are best accomplished in small groups of mothers in the unit before discharge. These groups should be informal and allow every mother an opportunity to contribute and to ask questions. When fathers are present, they should be included. These groups can be offered twice a day in most units and will save time and improve communications.

10. *Printed instructions.* Mothers have understandable difficulty remembering what they are told in the first twenty-four hours after the birth of their babies. During this period, instructions should be limited to a few important directions. To reinforce what they have been told, all parents should be given printed instructions when they are discharged.

Parents would do well to remember that this is *their* baby; their feelings and needs should have priority. Caregivers—whether a doctor, a midwife, a doula, or a nurse—are there to support this new family, answer the parents' questions, and encourage the nurturing talents built into the parents as human beings.

INFANT FEEDING AND THE

BEGINNING OF INTIMACY

A key moment for both breast- and bottle-feeding parents begins shortly after birth, with the first feeding. At this eventful time the mother and, usually, the father have their first glimpse at how a newborn manages on its own the vital functions of sucking, swallowing, and at the same time staying awake. We talk mostly about breast-feeding in the rest of the chapter because of the known physical, natural, and emotional benefits, but when women cannot breast-feed or choose not to, they need not feel guilty. Giving milk to one's infant in a bottle can also be a warm and loving experience for both parents. What is important is holding the infant in their arms and looking at the baby, so that feeding becomes a time for togetherness, rather than an impersonal experience.

Although breast-feeding is sometimes attempted immediately after birth, the first real breast-feeding works best when the mother and baby have rested a bit after the exhausting effort of labor and delivery. As mentioned in Chapter 4, if the mother has not received pain medication during labor and delivery, and the infant, after being thoroughly dried, is placed on the mother's chest and abdomen and is not disturbed (for routine care such as cleaning), the infant at thirty-five to fifty-five minutes of age typically will crawl vigorously to the mother's breast and nipple and then open his mouth widely and on his own begin to suckle on the areola (the brownish skin around the nipple).

The length of time for this astonishing event can vary. An experienced labor doula, who has helped more than a hundred women start breast-feeding shortly after delivery, has found that if the room is darkened and quiet, the newborn will often crawl and attach to the breast even sooner—ten to twenty minutes after the birth. If interrupted by lights or sound, the infant will pause for some time before resuming the movement to the breast.

The newborn can also accomplish this at a later time. The following comments from a mother whose healthy twins separately crawled from her abdomen to her breast on the day following birth convey the physical and emotional impact of the experience:

> The first feeling was related to the tremendous feeling of skin against skin. Immediately after their births, each of my daughters was whisked off fairly quickly, and it took a few moments before I could hold each child. By then, they had been skillfully wrapped in blankets. Having the opportunity later to place each baby naked on my abdomen was a powerful and reassuring feeling.
>
> As my daughter very slowly started to squirm and wiggle and roll up my abdomen towards one of my breasts, I was filled with a feeling of warmth and caring—a feeling of nurturing, a powerful feeling of mothering that I did not feel at

birth, although I had thought I would from all of the books that I read. I knew during this experience that we had really created these little humans. When she finally reached my nipple after the lengthy trip up my torso and tried to latch on, both my husband and I felt like cheering.

During this experience, I also felt wonder—wonder at the ability of our newborn daughters to coordinate their movements and instinctually direct themselves towards my breast. Every other movement we had seen was so uncoordinated that the ability to organize and somehow know where to go was miraculous.

On a more emotional note, I also felt a sense of reassurance. The first few days after birth were a complicated, confusing, and generally overwhelming time. Seeing each of my daughters complete this journey up my chest to my breast instilled confidence in me. In my mind, my new daughters had arrived in this world with a deep-seated and natural skill for survival and interest in being mothered. This talent my daughters had was terribly reassuring to me as a first-time mom. It was my hope (on some level) that I would have the correspondingly innate mothering skills that would help me during the difficult times.

At this first feeding and subsequent ones, the baby's own sensations of hunger should decide the timing. (This can be seen as the baby's very first step on the road to becoming independent.) Newborns usually signal their hunger by smacking their lips, increasing their saliva, turning their heads to find the nipple, and becoming more active. If these signals are not acted on after a short time, the newborn will begin to cry.

In this early sensitive time it is best that each mother be aware of certain important principles, such as finding a comfortable position, being sure that the lips of the infant are on the areola while the nipple is at the back of the infant's mouth (see Illustration 7), and being aware that in the first four to five minutes of suckling the infant receives 75 percent to 85 percent of the milk in a breast. Although most infants at birth know how to suckle, there is a remarkable improvement during the first days of life in their efficiency and skills in nursing. Infants quickly catch on to the mechanics, and the whole process begins to work more smoothly. While a supportive female caregiver—whether a nurse, a midwife, a doula, or an experienced family member—should be available for advice, such advice should not be intrusive. When left alone, the mother begins to find "her own baby" and learn the signals that tell her when the baby is sleepy, hungry, or satisfied.

As Winnicott notes:

> The mother's milk does not flow like an excretion. It is a response to a stimulus, and the stimulus is the sight and smell and feel of her baby and the sound of the baby's cry that indicates need. It is all one thing, the mother's care of her baby, and the periodic feeding develops as if it were a means of communication between the two—a song without words.[2]

During bottle- and breast-feeding, the infant is able to see the mother clearly, observe her facial expressions, and feel her warm body and arms. Interestingly, when a baby is feeding and the parents start talking, the baby often stops sucking or changes the sucking rate while trying to listen. Much silent communication occurs between parents and their infant. Holding, cuddling, soothing, sensing, and comforting one's baby during feeding are special experiences, and whether the baby is breast- or bottle-fed, this communication is present if the baby is held close in the parent's arms.

Mothers who breast-feed report that with each feeding, they feel a renewed sense of closeness, warmth, and love, and an increasing tie to their babies. Probably one component of this special feeling comes from the production of oxytocin, a natural substance that, as we mentioned in Chapter 4, is also called the "cuddle hormone." A baby's hunger cry, as well as its sucking on the nipple during lactation, leads to surges of oxytocin in the mother's circulation, which release milk from her breast. This hormone is also produced during labor and stimulates uterine contractions. In animal research, it has also been shown to activate pair bonding in small mammals and bonding behaviors between parent animals and their young.

It has been known for some time that breast milk is a rich source of antibodies, particularly in the colostrum (early milk). Breast milk and colostrum both contain high concentrations of secretory A immunoglobins, which coat the lining of the infant's intestine with a multitude of antibodies against infectious agents to which the mother has been exposed over her lifetime. As an example, if a mother has had a recent gastrointestinal infection with a salmonella bacteria before delivery, cells in the mother's intestinal lining will begin to produce antibodies against this organism. Some of these cells will migrate specifically to her mammary gland, where some will be discharged into the colostrum, and others will remain in the gland and produce antibodies against the salmonella, which the baby is likely to encounter during his journey through the birth canal and in the early months of life. These antibodies will protect the infant from developing a salmonella infection as long as he is breast-feeding. Similar protection is provided against many other potentially dangerous organisms in the environment. This explains in part how a newborn infant who is 100 percent breast-fed is protected in precarious environments from many infectious agents, both viral and bacterial, that can cause diarrhea and respiratory infections. In addition, in later years it appears that breast-fed infants have less chance of developing either diabetes or a chronic intestinal disorder called regional ileitis.

A recent British study of premature infants has shown other surprising advantages. Premature infants who were fed breast milk for just five weeks from a weight of two and a half to three and a half pounds had an IQ at eight years of age that was ten points higher than that of bottle-fed prematures.[3] In another exciting study, full-term infants fed only breast milk who were studied at four months of age were able to see smaller objects than formula-fed full-term infants, although by eight months their visual acuity was similar.[4]

The increased focus among childbirth professionals on early breast-feeding is also in part related to new knowledge about the physiology of breast-feeding. As an example, seven out of nine studies of early breast-feeding demonstrated that if a mother who wants to breast-feed suckles her infant in the first hour of life, she will more frequently succeed and will also nurse for a longer period of time.[5] Swedish investigators have observed that a mother will keep her infant in her room longer in the first four days of life if the infant's lips touch the mother's nipple in the first hour of life.[6]

A major error was made around 1900 by physicians when they regulated the schedule of feedings to just 6 feedings every 24 hours. Only in the past couple of decades has this advice been thoroughly repudiated. It has been shown that increasing the number of feedings from 6 to 10 or 11 feedings per 24 hours markedly decreases the bilirubin level (or yellow pigment) in the infant's blood—often lowering it to levels that eliminate concern about jaundice.[7] Increasing the feeding frequency also significantly decreases nipple soreness and breast tenderness, and most importantly, increases the mother's output of milk from 500 milliliters (17 ounces) which is almost adequate, to 750 milliliters (25 ounces) per 24 hours, which is a plentiful supply in the first weeks of life.[8] While 10 to 11 breast-feedings may sound like a marathon to a new mother, it is important to realize that this does not necessarily mean feeding every 2 hours. Since the majority of the milk from a breast is taken by a baby in the first 4 to 5 minutes of suckling, it is common for infants to feed for 5 to 8 minutes, then go to sleep for 10 to 15 minutes, awaken, and be interested in suckling again on the other breast. Each period of suckling separated by sleep for a period of 5 to

10 minutes of no suckling is considered a separate breast-feeding. Thus, it is possible to group the 10 to 11 feedings into a manageable schedule. As an example, 3 feedings might be between 6:00 and 7:00 P.M., with 4 to 5 hours of sleep, and then another group of 2 to 3 feedings, with a long period of sleep. The infant's own signals of hunger, however, must be the guiding factor.

To increase milk output, as well as success and comfort in breast-feeding, a mother can gradually increase the number of feedings each day, which is a much more effective approach than the rigid schedule advised in the past. Individual babies may need more feedings, and each mother must watch and listen to the needs of her particular baby. Some babies need more sucking, not only for nourishment but for comfort and closeness. This is called nonnutritive sucking. If this occurs on the breast and is comfortable for the mother and baby, it may also result in more milk production. However, the process of good milk production comes from increasing the number of feedings, not necessarily their duration. The more frequent the demand from the baby on the breast, the more the milk that is produced. In the early weeks, by following the baby's signals for nursing, a mother can usually balance out supply and demand and find a comfortable schedule that works for her and her baby. Increasing the feeding frequency also increases infant weight gain[9] and decreases the chance that the mother will ovulate.

As with early contact, the evident advantage of breast-feeding should not make mothers who cannot breast-feed feel guilty. Some women who cannot breast-feed their infants starting at birth, because of their own medical condition or a need for medication that precluded breast-feeding, may feel as though they are depriving their infants of something vital or are injuring their future relationship. But their infants' health and the mother–infant bond can be sustained in many ways. Since babies thrive on formula, it is often the mother's need that must be addressed. One mother in our practice, having been temporarily on a medication that precluded breast-feeding, explored with us her feelings of loss. In talking about this, she recognized that her worry about the baby being "deprived" was related to her own feeling of missing this early experience and not the baby's "need" for breast milk. Once free of her anxiety about this, she could see that her baby was doing well. This particular mother was still eager to attempt to breast-feed, even at a later date. She used a procedure developed for adoptive mothers and for mothers of premature babies. Formula in a plastic bag is hung over the mother's shoulder and drips through a tiny tube placed adjacent to the mother's nipple. Whenever suckling, the baby gets the formula needed and at the same time stimulates the breast to begin to produce milk. This mother was able to reestablish a milk supply over the next two and a half weeks so that the apparatus and formula could be discontinued. Other mothers in the same situation have found that extra cuddling during and after bottle-feeding and close contact with their babies leads to a closeness as deep and rewarding as any developed while breast-feeding.

It is helpful to reduce stress for breast-feeding mothers, since the release of milk from the breast can be altered by the mother's emotions. Breast-milk production can be reduced by worry about the infant's health or intake of milk, by conflict in personal relationships, or by a failure to get helpful advice to work out feeding problems. These issues are usually resolved with some encouragement and emotional support, opportunities to talk through concerns, and consistent breast-feeding advice.

As an example, many a young mother has been confused by well-meaning advice from older women who formula-fed their babies and who worry that breast-feeding may not be adequate for the baby. Grandmothers, with all good intentions, often express these concerns. They worry that there is no way to measure the amount of milk the baby is receiving. They also worry that their daughters and daughters-in-law will be tied to the baby and not receive adequate rest. Young parents often do not know how to counter this advice, for fear of showing disrespect to their mothers.

By becoming knowledgeable about breast-feeding and clear about what is important to them, parents can find the confidence and inner strength to do what they really want.

We are fortunate that in every area of the country there are well-trained lactation consultants who can quickly solve most problems. In addition, women who have learned relaxation techniques in preparation for labor can put these same exercises to good use for breast-feeding. Mothers of premature infants can produce more breast milk by using relaxation and visualization techniques that induce a feeling of calm, comfort, and confidence.[10] In general, relaxation techniques can help all mothers, whether breast- or bottle-feeding, to reduce some of the daily stress of motherhood.

This entire intricate interaction involving the baby's sucking—which affects the mother's hormones, activates a milk letdown response, enhances warm maternal feelings, and deepens sensitivity and love—continues an age-old human cycle. The fulfillment and gratification that occur for the infant during feeding may also be a beginning template for rewarding social and intimate relationships later in life.

6

DEVELOPING TIES: THE FIRST DAYS AND WEEKS

In the hospital, when we visit a mother the morning after she has given birth, we often find her looking bright-eyed, enthusiastic, loving, and cheerful. Her husband typically is attentive and may plan to stay home the first three days after the mother and baby return. Sometimes, the mother's mother or some other helper is expected to be there for the first week. Three weeks later, when the mother and baby arrive for the first checkup, the mother often appears tired, pale, and unkempt. She may bring many concerns: "My baby has no regular sleep pattern. I think he cries more than babies should. I have to get up two or three times every night to feed him. I am exhausted. I had no idea it was going to be so hard. It took me over three hours to get him ready to come in for this checkup."

NURTURING THE MOTHER

Women need to be nurtured long after childbirth. Today's mother goes home shortly after giving birth—twenty-four to forty-eight hours. When first-time mothers routinely spent five to seven days in the hospital, the entire hospital staff was familiar with the reactions of the mothers and their needs and set up classes to prepare them for the care of their babies at home. "Baby blues," occurring in 80 percent to 90 percent of normal women on the second or third day, were expected. Usually a mother had passed through this period before taking her baby home. There used to be time in the hospital (or in earlier days, at home births) for nurses, other mothers, or helpers to protect women and their babies during this period—to provide help and to offer caring role models and a sympathetic, experienced ear. Today the mother is whisked home, perhaps with a short period of some help—and then she is on her own, typically to cook, to clean, and to care for the baby. The expectation is that she is capable of doing it all.

When first-time parents come home from the hospital with their new infant, they embark on a task for which they have little preparation or experience. Despite the expectation of competency implied by current hospital practices, the need for support does not stop at the moment of birth. While almost all societies have had a system for helping parents through this period, some countries—including the United States—have lost the customs and arrangements that once had this effect. Today, the lack of a widely accepted cultural tradition for giving the necessary support after childbirth puts many families at risk. In the past a mother's mother and other female relatives provided this assistance and guidance. But today the mother's mother is often at work, and there may be no one to fill the void.

It is often difficult for a new mother to recognize her needs and feelings and give herself permission to ask for help. Usually, neither parent has a good understanding of an infant's needs and therefore cannot anticipate the endless demands of a newborn child. To shift from an active life with social and work contacts and a large number of friendly and supportive associates to meeting the never-ending demands of a young infant, alone at home, is a momentous change. The burden of continuous responsibility with no letup and the unusual and unexpected degree of fatigue can make a mother feel desperate about whether she can survive and how she will manage.

The small amount of time that the American mother has with her infant in the hospital means that they are not fully acquainted at the time of discharge. The first days at home are described by many mothers as the most difficult days of their lives. Often the mother's idea of what a "good mother" should be able to accomplish with her baby has been built up to such an unrealistic level by magazine articles or books of advice that she may exhaust herself trying and then have little tolerance for the many minor problems that naturally arise during the early care of her infant.

In the nonindustrialized societies that we have studied, the mother and baby are placed together, with support, protection, and isolation from other demands and people, for at least seven days— and sometimes for weeks—after birth. In rural China, for instance, the custom has been to have such a period for forty days.

One of the authors' recent patients who delivered a full-term, healthy baby provides an example of the postpartum care traditionally provided in another culture. This woman's mother came from India in time for the delivery and took care of everything. The new mother stayed in bed during the first forty days, and except for brief periods, she and her infant were not separated. The new mother did not go out with the baby because of concern about germs, but she did have family visitors. She was cared for like a queen. Every day she was massaged thoroughly with sesame oil, and the baby was massaged with warm olive oil. The grandmother had brought from India a large box of herbs, seeds, and crushed nuts. The mother ate this delicious mixture all day to produce good milk for her baby, and she was also given a mixture of milk and crushed almonds sweetened with honey, as well as other special foods to help her body recuperate and to enhance the quality and quantity of milk. In India, many mothers and their babies receive this type of support and protection from either a family member or a close friend.

In many industrialized societies in Europe, parental leave is provided, ranging from a minimum of three months to a year or more. Often the leave involves full pay for part of this time, and in some countries the father and mother can share this leave. In addition, many services are provided for the mother and infant. For example, in England daily visits are made by health visitors for the first fourteen days after a mother and baby are discharged from the hospital. These health visitors help bathe the baby, check on the condition of the mother and baby, answer questions, and arrange for additional services when special situations arise. In Holland, if a mother delivers at home, a baby nurse stays with her for ten days postpartum to help around the house. These services are made available to all mothers. In recognition of the importance of mothers and their babies, the government provides additional funds and services to all mothers during pregnancy and the period of infancy. (In Finland the amount is about $2,300.) These are useful models to consider, in view of the enormous benefits to the health of the family.

In contrast, the following are some recent comments from mothers and fathers in the United States whom we have talked with during the postpartum period. "I walked in from work [five days after the baby's birth]," said one father, "and found my wife was just sitting there crying. She feels she is a lousy mother, the house is dirty, and she is afraid to bathe the baby." "After three days home we realized we were going to be twenty-four-hour parents with no vacations, and we were already exhausted." One mother was heard to say, "My mom is leaving in three days, and I don't know if I can manage as well as she can." "I know he [a one-week-old] is just a baby; I shouldn't get angry at him." "My wife is always so tired, I'm beginning to worry about our relationship. Will we ever be close again?" "I don't think the baby likes me." "I don't think I can get time alone." At three months, a mother said, "Our sex life [three months after the baby was born] is terrible. Is the problem with me or with him or with us?"

As part of our research, we recently asked a large number of mothers to comment on any problems during the postnatal stay in the hospital. Almost every mother answered, "I have not had time to get to know my baby, and to know what to do with my baby at home." Our maternity unit in Cleveland reports that currently the hospital is receiving a large number of telephone requests for classes to help new parents learn about caring for their baby. The parents say they are poorly prepared for this task. There are exceptions, of course. A first-time mother with considerable experience caring for younger siblings or babysitting with young infants may well be happy, competent, and confident in her care of her own infant and know how to handle the common problems.

A MAJOR LIFE CHANGE

The birth of a baby inevitably results in physical changes for the mother and emotional and lifestyle changes for both parents. This is particularly the case with the birth of the first baby. Continuous responsibility for a helpless human being can be an overwhelming experience. On top of this comes a major change in relationships. The twosome has become a threesome, and the mother is now drawn compellingly into a relationship with the baby, even though she may be trying to maintain the same relationship she previously had with her partner. The birth also results in a major change in the role and responsibilities of the new father. Starting with the baby's first cry, it is common for fathers to feel an enhanced concern and anxiety about meeting the financial needs of the family. For both parents, the euphoria associated with the birth of the new baby is soon pushed aside by tensions about meeting the baby's needs, maintaining a relationship with each other, and making adjustments from the former activities of the twosome to the new realities.

The joy of becoming parents is accompanied by what the writer Judith Viorst calls "necessary losses": loss of the exclusive relationship with the partner, loss of many of the activities the parents participated in together, loss of the daily contacts with colleagues (for the parent who remains at home with the baby), changes in educational plans and job prospects, loss of income. These many changes and new responsibilities for both father and mother, plus multiple hormonal changes in the mother, may cause emotions to go up and down.

There may be other losses around the birth, including a loss of choice or independence, and feelings about unfulfilled expectations may arise. There may be anger and dissatisfaction over the birth experience itself that are never expressed but that come out later, in the care of the baby or in the relationship to the spouse. For parents with more than one child, there may be a sense of separation from the other child. The triggering at birth of memories about difficult past birth experiences sometimes results in anger or sadness. If a previous neonatal loss has not been worked through, the anger, sadness, grief, and expectations associated with the lost infant can be mixed with thoughts about the new baby. The birth of a baby brings a number of abrupt developmental changes, including needing to see oneself as an adult and parent and having to give up the thought that one's parents will always be there. For young parents, it is now their turn to look after others. Parents may feel pulled by conflicting needs to act as responsible adults and to seek family and emotional supports. This may trigger old dependency needs for the father or mother who must strike a delicate balance between a need for selfhood and a need for support.

PRIMARY MATERNAL PREOCCUPATION

Not long ago, a graduate student came to one of the authors with her two-month-old for a checkup. She said, "I don't know what's the matter. I have always been known as an efficient student. I always got my work done, and I have been able to do some research on the side. My advisor asked me to write up part of my studies that I know well. I was planning to take two months to be at home with the baby, so I said, 'Sure, I can do that easily.' The baby is beautiful and hasn't been sick. In three days those two months will be up, and I haven't had time to write a word."

This complete focus on the new infant has been described by D. W. Winnicott as "primary maternal preoccupation."[1] He noted that in the perinatal period there is a special mental state of the mother in which she has a greatly increased sensitivity to, and focus upon, the needs of her baby. Such a state begins toward the end of the pregnancy and continues for a few weeks after the birth of the child. To develop and maintain this state, a mother needs support, nurturing, and a protected environment.

This unique preoccupation and the openness to the baby that it engenders in the mother are key factors in the bonding process. "Only if a mother is sensitized in the way I am describing," wrote Winnicott, "can she feel herself into her infant's place, and so meet the infant's needs." In Chapters 4 and 5, we have seen many examples of the special sensitivity of the mother in picking up the subtle signals of her infant. As we will see in Chapter 7, this is true whether the baby is fragile, tiny, and premature or robust, healthy, and full-term.

Winnicott described how a mother shows love to her infant through physical and emotional holding, a "holding environment," which is crucial for the child's physical and emotional development. He felt that mothers develop this capacity by being supported and cared for themselves in a way that recognizes their important maternal task.

Just as the hormonally produced sleepiness and fatigue in the first three months of pregnancy may result in the mother resting more and providing a more favorable environment for the fetus when the vital organs are being formed, so also the hormonal changes and the state of "primary maternal preoccupation" in the first weeks after delivery enhance the mother's ability to sense and to meet the needs of her new infant in what has been called the fourth trimester. This state preoccupies new mothers so much that they are often unable to carry out other tasks (such as the graduate student's writing assignment).

After a mother has a baby, her mind tends to go back to an early time in her life. These memories may evoke in her a special need to be protected. As part of this psychological regression, a mother needs to feel safe, to be held, and to be cared for. When this need is not met, a woman may feel abandoned, lonely, and insecure. In our culture the husband's support is essential for a mother, but he has similar needs during this period. Emotional and practical support for both needs to continue after the birth.

A FATHER'S NEW ROLE

Despite changes in our society, we tend to agree with Winnicott that fathers' and mothers' roles are not interchangeable, as we noted earlier. A father, said Winnicott,[2]

can provide a space in which the woman has elbow room. Properly protected the mother is saved from having to turn outward to deal with her surroundings at the time when she is wanting so much to turn inward, when she is longing to be concerned with the inside of the circle which she can make with her arms in the center of which is the baby. This period of time in which the mother is naturally preoccupied with the one infant does not last long. The mother's bond with the baby is very powerful at the beginning and we must do all we can to enable her to be preoccupied with her baby at this time—the natural time.

The complexities of this new era of changing relationships and roles were brought home to us by the following case. Before their baby was born, a young professional couple had worked out a program of coparenting. After participating in a successful birth experience and while the wife was getting breast-feeding established, the father complained with some anger that his only role was in the "chores" of baby care—the changing and dressing and bathing—and that his wife had all the "fun" of feeding—something he could not do. The wife, on the other hand, commented that all she could do was "feed" the baby, when her husband had all the other "pleasures" of changing, bathing, and caregiving. After a long discussion, they realized that they were competing to see who had the hardest task and who had the most pleasure. Realizing that these roles were equally vital and, in any case, immeasurable, they could laugh about their feelings.

A subsequent baby may bring different stressors for the family as the adults make concerted efforts to coparent. In another case the parents had worked out joint responsibili-ties with their first infant. When the second planned baby was born, the mother expected the father to pitch in as before. At this time the father, however, was in a more stressful situation at work. He felt an overload of responsibility in adding new baby care to his already burdened schedule, which included time with his first child, who was still a toddler. Their arrangement was that he would take care of the infant after feedings by his wife, and soothe or amuse the baby until the next feeding or sleeptime. He began to be unsure about whether the baby's fussing was still related to being hungry or just needing holding, and he resented having to be the only one to decide. Since he had been so tuned in with the first baby, his wife could not understand why he was having so much trouble, and she began to believe that he was rejecting the baby. When they started talking about the situation, it was apparent that he did not believe he could complain about the extra burden he felt without having his wife feel unloved or invalidated as a mother. Describing his dismay about how time-consuming and demanding a second baby proved to be was a "forbidden subject." Once he was able to communicate his feelings, he and his wife were able to resolve the situation. These issues may seem minor, but such disagreements are common and may drive a wedge between the couple unless they are discussed and resolved.

A particularly important role for the father is to act as an intermediary with the outside world. We have observed repeatedly that if the mother is protected and can sleep when the baby sleeps and not become overly tired or exhausted, her experience with the baby during the postpartum period may proceed relatively smoothly. The desire of many relatives and friends to visit and the need to feed and entertain them often result in the mother's exhaustion and fatigue. The mother often rushes to provide refreshments to visitors who sometimes stay until late in the evening and then go home to sleep while the mother herself is just starting her night duties. Politeness is desirable at times, but in the postpartum period it can result in the mother's undoing. In such cases, the father can be the guardian of the door and telephone. He can say on the phone that his wife has been getting up with the baby at night and is now sleeping and that she will call back, or he can tell unplanned visitors that it would be helpful if they could come a few days later for a short time. If it does not seem appropriate to say this, we advise him to have them come in, but tell them that his wife will only be able to come by to say hello to them briefly. While this sounds a bit harsh, if the parents use this as the general plan, they can modify it for special visitors and the condition of the mother. The mother and father should talk about what her choice would be and realize that this may need to be modified, depending on the sleeping pattern of the baby and the progress with feedings.

For couples to bear up under the fatigue, the role and work changes, and the disruption of eating, sleeping, sex, and social activities, each partner needs to make a major effort at being understanding, supportive, and communicative (see Illustration 8). It is hard to imagine just how tired parents can become when their baby's feeding schedules and needs do not follow any normal day-night cycle. Taking turns with the "nighttime watch" can help, but it is equally important for a couple to express their feelings. A father needs to be aware of the strain on the mother's system after giving birth. Couples do best if they already communicate well before the baby is born, if they have similar ideas about parenting, and if the father has truly wanted the baby. If conflicts arise, the couple can benefit from discussing these feelings and differences with an objective person, such as a counselor or other professional.

Fathers' needs are sometimes also related to their own experiences. A father in the practice of one of the authors described how he did not feel close to his baby and did not believe he was competent to take care of him. He revealed that he had never known his father and had been raised in foster homes, as well as an orphanage. He had no model of how to be a father and needed help and encouragement to find the nurturing part of himself to give to his child. As it turned out, he was already responding lovingly to his baby without realizing it. He gained confidence and delight by discovering the responsiveness of his own baby as we performed a version of the Brazelton Neonatal Assessment Scale. During this he could watch his baby turn toward a sound and follow his father's face. He could see that the baby responded and was actively seeking his attention. The void that he had felt as a child could start to be filled and healed with the delicate, step-by-step interaction created between him and his son.

Fathers such as this one benefit greatly from meeting with groups of other fathers in the same way that mothers in groups share common feelings, concerns, and methods of how to interact with their babies. Fathers also begin to develop a closeness with their baby if they have time alone in the first hours of life (Illustration 6).

THE PROBLEM OF EXPECTATIONS

In the hectic atmosphere of a modern hospital, the heightened sensitivity of primary maternal preoccupation is sometimes misinterpreted by physicians and nurses as excessive anxiety. Once the parents are at home, the importance of this period may still not be sufficiently recognized. Mothers have *expectations* of being perfect mothers—handling baby, work, and life as usual—and fathers need their wives to be back to normal quickly, back to handling home, job, and their usual relationship. When this does not occur, a mother may feel guilty, and a father may be critical and unsympathetic. The following is a good example of a mother who put heavy demands on herself for perfection.

A creative teacher in a busy day-care center had felt competent and confident at pursuing her employment and managing her home, but she was now overwhelmed by the tasks of new motherhood. She began to see herself as an inadequate mother. Together with the pain of an episiotomy, these feel-ings left her almost incapacitated. Choosing to stay at home to breast-feed and care for her baby while her partner was continuing as a full-time student and working, she had expected to cope more easily and was embarrassed and ashamed that she was feeling so bad. In this situation, she was experiencing the loss of her former identity as a competent working woman. She also needed to accept the reality that she could not—and did not have to—keep up with everything as perfectly as before. This was especially difficult for her because she had always had very high expectations of herself. In her role as a caregiver, she was not used to asking for or needing help. In talking about this situation, she recognized that she needed to mourn the loss of these former identities of herself, to give herself permission to take some time for herself, to learn how to ask for and receive help from her partner, to reach out to other parents (especially those with children) and friends, and to recognize that these were normal feelings and that she was not alone. In talking to some other mothers, she learned that all new mothers have these feelings of being overwhelmed at the beginning and that unrealistic expectations were a common problem, especially when one could be so efficient and competent in one's paid work. Baby schedules did not fit any time clock. Given a brief opportunity to talk through the situation and have her feelings clarified, this new mother was able to rethink her situation and work out a system that relieved her of these unrealistic and emotionally damaging expectations, and thereby avoid possible depression.

Many women feel distressed that they cannot do everything as easily as before, and wonder if life will ever return to normal. Sometimes a mother in this period may question her own desire to return to work:"I'm so in love with this baby, I never want to leave him. Will I ever want to go back to work? Is something the matter with me?" Women have even told us how they have held back on becoming fully attached to their babies because they knew they would have to go back to work soon, or because they had had such severe, sad, and upsetting reactions when they went back to school or work early with the previous baby that they did not want to go through this wrenching emotional reaction again.

As we try to understand the conflict between a mother's biological and psychological needs versus the demands of her culture, we often note two patterns: First, a large number of mothers need to work to maintain the family's finances or to meet their professional or personal goals. To do this, they may feel compelled to take less than the three months of parental leave that employers are now required to provide by law. As a result of the demands of their work and/or education, they hesitate to start breast-feeding or they want to discontinue it in the first month or two. Other mothers in the same situation manage to continue breast-feeding after they return to work or school and find that this enhances the development of their tie to their infants.

A second common experience is for mothers to plan to take a period of leave for the first two or three months. These mothers then become so enamored with their infants that they extend their parental leave to six months or beyond. They may comment, "This may keep me from graduating this year or from getting a raise, but I just can't bear to leave my new baby." These women have developed a strong, healthy tie to their infants before returning to their paid work. As we will see, this tie may actually make it easier to separate from the infant, because the mother is confident of the attachment. If expectations of performing perfectly both at home and at the workplace prevent a mother from allowing attachment to develop, the conflicted emotions may actually last longer.

POSTPARTUM DEPRESSION

It is important to distinguish between the normal "baby blues" and true depression. The baby blues mentioned earlier are characterized by a short period of volatile emotions, commonly occurring between the second and fifth postpartum days and affecting between 80 percent and 90 percent of new mothers. In contrast, the term *postpartum depression* refers to the symptoms described below, which usually begin at four to eight weeks postpartum (but sometimes, later in the first year) and which can persist for more than a year. The incidence ranges from 10 percent to 16 percent of new mothers. In the past, women with these symptoms rarely sought treatment, and women with severe cases were hospitalized. Postpartum psychosis, however, is rare.

The symptoms of postpartum depression cover a wide range, including irritability, frequent crying, feelings of helplessness and hopelessness, lack of energy and motivation so that the woman's ability to function is disturbed, lack of interest in sexual relations, disturbances of appetite and sleep, and feelings of being unable to cope with new demands. Anxiety, a very frequent feature, is often related to the infant's welfare and may persist in spite of reassurance by physicians and nurses. It shows up in some mothers as lack of affection for the baby and, in turn, self-blame and guilt. Expectations again play a role here. Mothers may be concerned that they are not able to measure up to their own image of the ideal mother. It is not uncommon for a woman suffering from postpartum depression to have psychosomatic symptoms such as headache, backache, vaginal discharge, and abdominal pain for which no organic cause can be found. A mild appearance of one or more of these feelings is normal. Many mothers working to meet the demands of their new babies and missing sleep may find that some of these symptoms fit their own situation. When they are many and continue over a period of weeks, help is needed. The outlook for mothers suffering from postpartum depression is good if the diagnosis and treatment are started early. When there is a long delay in starting treatment, the depression may be prolonged. Often short-term psychotherapy is all that is needed. Simply having someone to talk to is very helpful in working out these symptoms. Depending on the individual circumstances, some women may also benefit from medication during this time. When symptoms are severe and go unabated, medication and even hospitalization may be necessary for a short period of time to give relief.

The case of a new mother whom we shall call Amy is a typical example of postpartum depression. Amy was referred for therapy because she was unusually anxious about her six-month-old baby, who checked out to be a healthy little boy. When Amy began talking about the baby, she could not stop crying. She described how sad and anxious she had been feeling in the past month. She had trouble doing any of her normal activities, had difficulty sleeping, and was not interested in resuming marital relations. She found it impossible to leave the baby. She worried that the baby would be emotionally hurt if she left even for a short time, but she also felt trapped by the baby's need for constant care. As she continued to express her feelings, she realized how angry she was at her husband, James, because she felt she did not receive the support she needed. Her husband believed that mothers were the best caregivers for babies, and he looked forward to being more involved when the child was a bit older. Amy had planned to resume employment by this time, but found that she could not trust anyone else with the baby.

As Amy continued to talk, it became clear that these feelings and symptoms had been lasting for more than a couple of weeks and that she was evidencing postpartum depression. Being listened to and having her feelings understood and validated were Amy's first steps toward treatment. It also helped her to learn about, give a name to, and normalize this postpartum condition. Learning that she was not "crazy," that this was a treatable problem, and that there were many things she could do to work through it gave her some relief.

Amy was helped to learn ways to structure her days, devote more time to her own care, set priorities, and learn some methods for relaxing and reducing stress. She needed to recognize the distorted thinking of self-blame and self-criticism and the vicious cycle of distorted, anxious thoughts about the baby so common to women with postpartum depression. She was encouraged to find constructive ways to recognize feelings of anger and express them. In therapy she realized how disappointed and angry she was at her husband for his lack of involvement, but she had held these feelings in because she did not want to anger or upset him. The feelings had gone underground so that she had turned them against herself. As she explored further, she became more aware that her mother had had maternal depression and that she, Amy, had somehow internalized this old way of responding, which had been retriggered now by the birth of her own baby. In individual therapeutic work, she needed to work through grief and loss and the trauma of the depression itself, as well as the unresolved issues from her past. By engaging her husband's help and joining a postpartum depression group, Amy gained the support she needed. Within a few months she was able to resume her normal life with new coping skills and a greater sense of self-affirmation.

Most studies have shown that a person's previous history or a family history of psychiatric problems increases the chances of postpartum depression. However, psychosocial factors are also very important. The effects of unfavorable life events or chronic problems such as bereavement, unemployment, inadequate income, unsatisfactory housing, or unsupportive relations may be intensified by the fact that the new mother feels trapped and unable to change her circumstances. The experience of childbirth may bring back to her the emotional reactions related to unresolved grief for the death of her own mother, or a poor relationship with her, or separation from one or both parents at an early age. In these cases, she is more likely to be depressed. A mother's inability to confide in her husband or a friend has been noted as a factor in depression. Women are often embarrassed to tell anyone how bad they feel. Loneliness, isolation, and lack of support are serious problems for today's mothers, especially when there is a large discrepancy between the idealization and the reality of motherhood.

EFFECT OF MATERNAL DEPRESSION ON AN INFANT

Postpartum depression can have serious implications for the young infant. A number of studies show an association between maternal depression and later developmental problems, including behavioral disturbances, physical ill health, insecure attachments, and symptoms of depression.[3] The symptoms of postpartum depression—irritability, anxiety, poor concentration, and depressive mood—interfere with all interpersonal relations, especially a mother's developing relationship with her new infant.

Infants are highly sensitive to the quality of adult attention. If normal mother–infant communication is disrupted for even brief periods, infants respond with distress and avoidance. In ingenious and dramatic experiments done at Boston Children's Medical Center, mothers of three- or four-month-old babies were asked to present a still, unresponsive, and expressionless face to their infants.[4] This would be followed by a dramatic change in the infants' appearance. In the first minute or two, the infants would smile, and wave and struggle to obtain a response from their mothers. After several unsuccessful efforts, they would become discouraged and often would begin to spit up. By three to four minutes their whole bodies slumped in despair. These were very brief experiments, followed by warm hugs, but it is easy to see that mothers' depression and unresponsiveness may be injurious to infants' development.

Therapy for maternal depression symptoms must also address the mother–infant relationship and any symptoms the infant may show. Because prevention is of primary importance, early diagnosis is the goal. In one study, the developmental-test performance at eighteen months of infants of depressed mothers showed significantly poorer results than did that of infants of new mothers who had never been depressed. Infants whose mothers had been depressed in the postnatal period were significantly more likely to be insecurely attached at eighteen months than infants of nondepressed mothers.[5] It is important to emphasize that maternal problems frequently show up as infant problems, such as crying, spitting up, or feeding difficulties.

Recognizing postpartum depression is thus important not only for the understanding and treatment of the mother, but also because of its negative effects on the relationship between the mother and the baby, and on the child's learning and social and emotional development. Prevention of postpartum depression is the best way to avoid such effects, and social support is one of the most vital factors in prevention.

RECOMMENDATIONS

1. *Planning ahead.* Ideally, planning for a support system for the mother, father, and family should be carried out well before the new baby is expected. Because of work situations, certain discomforts of pregnancy, and some uncertainties about the birth, many parents find it difficult to settle on arrangements until labor begins or the baby is born. Unfortunately, the short stay in the hospital does not provide new parents with enough time to make many of the valuable, crucial arrangements for support.

2. *Protecting the mother.* A mother needs help and a sheltered environment for at least three to four weeks so she can establish a rewarding rhythmic interaction with her baby and establish the infant's feedings.

3. *Postpartum help.* Today many husbands or partners arrange for one or two weeks of vacation to help the mothers get started with the baby, but they vary greatly in their ability to manage the household. Even though they may live far away, a mother's mother and mother-in-law may be able to provide help for a few days. However, many middle-aged women are employed, so it is almost impossible for them to provide the month or so of support that would be most beneficial. The support (cooking, cleaning, caring for the baby while the mother sleeps) provided by the husband, a sister, a mother, or a friend—if only for a week—is not to be underrated, but such a short period of support does make it difficult for the mother to feel protected and able to devote herself almost completely to becoming acquainted with her new baby. We urge parents to plan ahead for postpartum home help. A teenage girl or older woman for three hours a day three to five days a week can remarkably improve the life of the parents and baby. There is considerable evidence that providing support at this special time in a mother's life may decrease feelings of depression. In many cities in our country, postpartum doulas are available through the National Association of Postpartum Care Services (NAPCS), 8910 299th Place SW, Edmonds, Washington, 98026.

4. *Support of both parents.* Just as the labor doula, during birth, provides emotional support and encouragement to the father and shows him how to be most helpful to his wife, so also should whoever provides support in the household—whether a relative, a friend or a postpartum doula—keep the couple and their relationship in mind.

5. *Single mothers.* When babies are born to a single-parent household, the need for support may be greater. If the single mother has a good relationship with and support from her family, the first weeks may be a period of relatively smooth transition. On the other hand, if she is struggling alone, or is separated geographically or estranged from her family, then there is a compelling need for the assistance of a support person for the welfare of the mother, the baby, and their relationship.

6. *Breast-feeding support.* With early discharge, the systems established in maternity hospitals to help mothers start breast-feeding have been truncated, and additional services obviously are often needed. In most communities there are women who have had success with breast-feeding who can be helpful and supportive to a new mother. Often, there are also lactation consultants in most communities. Many mothers have found it helpful to see a lactation consultant before the birth of the baby, both to prevent future problems and to have someone to call when urgent questions arise. After one or two visits by a lactation consultant, many mothers who were on the verge of discontinuing breast-feeding have had an extremely rewarding breast-feeding experience. In addition, the La Leche League usually is also able to provide useful answers and, if necessary, the names of expert women to consult with.

7. *Infant crying.* When infant crying becomes stressful for parents, they may find that carrying the baby about in a Snugli-type carrier may be helpful. When three-week-old infants are carried for three extra hours a day, at times unrelated to crying or feeding, studies have shown 50 percent less crying (particularly in the evening hours) than a group who had not been carried the extra three hours.[6] This decreased crying and fussing were shown to be associated with generally increased contentment in the first three months of life. Another study that involved second-by-second observations of healthy infants in their homes, showed that if a mother intervened within ninety seconds after a baby began to cry, the crying would stop quickly. However, if she waited more than a minute and a half to respond, a prolonged period of calming was often necessary before the crying ceased.[7]

8. *Parent groups.* Many mothers and fathers have been helped by participating in parent groups—most commonly, mothers in groups with other mothers—to discuss the problems they have encountered with their babies and to hear about solutions found by these other parents.

9. *Realistic expectations.* Parents should not push themselves to keep everything as perfect as before. We remind parents to give themselves permission for rest, time-outs, and brief pleasurable outings and to let go of those "gold standards" of household or other work at this time.

10. *Time to communicate.* The relationship between the parents must be given priority, to keep communication open. It is important for parents to talk often with each other about their feelings and needs. A "five-minute rule" may be helpful. That is, each evening one partner takes five minutes to speak to the other about feelings and concerns of the day, while the other partner just listens attentively. After five minutes the process is reversed so each one receives a turn. This is a time for supportive *listening*, not criticizing, analyzing, or advising.

11. *Relaxation techniques.* It is extremely useful to learn relaxation and stress-management techniques. For some parents, visualization, meditation, and relaxation breathing techniques help; other people prefer physical activity to reduce stress. Physiological and mental relaxation processes (such as imagery and self-hypnosis) are especially helpful to reduce tension on a daily basis. One cannot be relaxed and tense at the same time.

7

PREMATURE BIRTH
AND BONDING

When we and other investigators began to study the ways in which the parents of a premature baby manage to form a relationship with their immature, sleepy, unpredictable, fragile infant, we noted many common adaptations, problems, and detours. In recent years a great deal has been learned about the complex and confusing ecology parents encounter when the birth of a premature or sick infant brings them into an intensive care nursery. This chapter attempts to place in perspective the innovative work of the nurses, physicians, and psychologists who have broken down the walls of the intensive care unit to allow parents to form close attachments to their premature babies.

In contrast to the euphoric moments together that they had expected, parents of premature babies first come to know them in a hectic world of harassed, overworked nurses and physicians, other overwhelmed parents, and critically sick infants. However, new knowledge of perinatal and neonatal care, coupled with the desire to apply these latest ideas to benefit premature infants and their families, has made premature nurseries a more humane place. There has also been increasing interest in the developmental abilities and characteristics of premature newborns and their interaction with their families when they are home.

During the same period, remarkable strides have been made in improving both the survival rate and quality of life of very small premature babies. When all the modern techniques—which include early fluid and nutrition administration, special respiratory care when necessary, and close and detailed monitoring of oxygen, environmental temperature, pH, respiration, and heart rate—are employed, a premature infant of over three and a half pounds can do almost as well as a full-term infant. Advances in obstetrical and neonatal care and technology have gradually led to a measurable improvement in the quality of survival for even the smallest of low-birth-weight infants. For example, in the last eight to ten years in an optimal hospital setting, approximately 85 percent to 90 percent of surviving infants weighing between two and three pounds were free from significant mental or physical handicaps.

The survival of even very immature infants (one and a half to two pounds) has also improved so that nearly 65 percent to 90 percent of these infants survive with the use of lung surfactant, modern respiratory techniques, and the ability to give most of the infants nutrition intravenously. If birth weight is between two and a half and three and a half pounds, the survival rate is around 94 percent; between one and a half and two and a half pounds, 65 percent to 85 percent; and between one and one and a half pounds, 30 percent to 50 percent. Neonatologists and the other members of these units now assume that with meticulous attention to the baby's well-being before, during, and after birth, 90 percent of premature infants weighing more than two pounds will survive intact—an optimistic attitude that makes a focus on psychological well-being and support for parents all the more vital.

A PARENT'S FIRST REACTIONS TO THE BIRTH OF A PREMATURE INFANT

A parent's first concern is for the infant's survival. Feelings of guilt heighten feelings of anxiety. Parents fear that some-thing they did or did not do during their pregnancy affected the baby and resulted in the prematurity. Years before parents were allowed to visit the premature nursery, a sensitive caregiver stressed that it is essential for the mother to see the premature baby as soon as possible after birth to help "minimize the frightening fantasies which she may develop and help her to begin the process of handling any 'emotional lag.'"[1] He defined "emotional lag" as the alienation of feeling that a new mother can experience during her early relationship with a premature baby. The "difficulty in experiencing the warm, maternal feelings which she expected" is not confined to mothers of premature infants but may be equally intense anytime mothers are denied close contact with their full-term infants.

Others have viewed the reactions of mothers to the birth of a premature infant in the context of an acute reaction to trauma. This approach sees premature birth as a crisis, as a "time-limited period of disequilibrium or behavioral and subjective upsets to which the person is temporarily unable to respond adequately. During this period of tension the person grapples with the problem and develops novel resources, both by calling upon internal reserves and making use of the help of others. Those resources are then used to handle the precipitating factor and the person achieves once more a steady state."[2] Reactions to a stressful event, such as the birth of a premature infant, can also be heavily conditioned by previously existing personality factors.

In the first hours of her infant's life, one mother expressed to us many common thoughts of mothers of premature babies: "I was really shocked. I was tired out and I hadn't seen my baby, and all I could think of was, 'My baby's very sick and they're going to take her away.' I was really afraid she wasn't going to be with me very long. I was ready to run down to the nursery. You know they don't want you to get out of bed right away and you're supposed to take it easy after delivery. I got out of bed, and the nurse came in and said, 'You can't get out of bed,' and I said, 'Well, then, you'll have to get me a wheelchair because I'm going down there and I'm going to see my baby because they're taking her away.' So they took me down there, and she looked terrible. I thought, 'Oh, my poor little baby.' "

Now that parents are permitted into special care nursery units, caregivers have tried to discover what being in such a nursery means to parents. The anthropologist, L. F. Newman defined certain key questions:[3] What is the role of parents whose infant is cared for entirely or largely by others? In the professionals' workplace, with all the stresses of intensive care, how do these parents cope with the presumed or potential tragedies of the infants surrounding them and the unknown destiny of their own child?

Using anthropological techniques, Newman noted variations between families and even within families that reflected individual coping styles and personal adaptations to the stress of a premature birth. "Coping through commitment" is one style—an intense, yet variable, involvement in the care of a low-birth-weight infant. "Coping through distance" is another—a slower acquaintance process, in which parents rely on the care provided by experts and express fear, anxiety, and at times denial before they accept the surviving infant.

The families of premature infants are subject to extraordinary pressures. "For the parents time seems both to slip away yet remain frozen in place. Geographically displaced, their work and lives disrupted, their biological rhythms in disarray, bewildered, anxious, and terribly tired, parents in the delirium of crisis are simply unable to comprehend what is happening."[4]

ADJUSTING TO THE BIRTH

We discussed earlier how the mother of a normal, healthy newborn must adjust her idealized image of her infant to the actual infant before her. Naturally, this is much more difficult for the parents of a premature infant. They must reconcile their idealized mental picture with a wan, scrawny, and feeble-appearing infant. Because the parents of a premature infant have difficulty recognizing that their tiny baby will ultimately grow into a normal, husky, vigorous, healthy youngster, coming to terms with his appearance is far from easy.

The average mother who comes to visit her infant is not prepared physically or emotionally for the early birth, and is still shaky from it. She is extremely anxious about her baby's health; wonders about any abnormalities; worries about whether she will be criticized for producing an unfinished, fragile, imperfect baby; and fears that she may carry germs which will harm the infant. She enters the brightly lit, stainless steel and glass citadel, filled with unfamiliar sounds and smells, and densely populated by intense men and women who rush from incubator to incubator, manipulate complicated equipment, and spend long periods hovering over individual babies. These activities appear ominous and suggest an air of great tension—even after several visits. It is not until she has been told that her baby is definitely progressing well or, far better, until she has touched and seen the child herself, that the mother can begin to relax.

At each visit a new problem may be discovered or announced, and with every problem the mother feels a sharp visceral pain. "Do babies on a respirator live?" "How will she ever stand the strain of breathing so hard when she is already so small and fragile?" "Does such a tiny thing ever grow up to be a full-sized child or adult?" "Are they telling me the truth?" "What have I done to my poor child?" Parents must feel free to ask such questions and to express concerns to health professionals. They must also be able to have confidence in the answers they receive. Communication between everyone involved in the care of a premature or sick infant is a daily necessity.

As an example, many small or sick infants are transported from the hospital where they are born to a hospital with an intensive care unit. At the time of transfer, even if the infant is being moved only for observation of an elevated bilirubin level, parents are understandably worried about their infant's survival, and will often require additional support. Therefore, in our work, before the infant is transported, we show the baby to his mother and father and attempt to describe to the parents, in simple terms, the care their baby will receive. We ask the father to help us care for his infant, impressing on him that he has a very special role to play. There are really two individuals in his family needing care—his wife, in one part of the hospital (or at home or in another hospital), and his baby, in the neonatal center. In addition, the father sometimes has responsibility for other children at home. We have observed that, by bringing him into the situation early, he can better master his own anxieties. For these reasons we suggest that he come to the intensive care nursery and discuss the baby's condition with the physicians and nurses and familiarize himself with the routine before visiting his wife. In this way he can discuss current information with his wife and help to allay her fears. If his wife is still in the maternity hospital for any reason, his visits to her will be even more important, though he may feel torn until she can join him in visiting the baby.

Before the mother's first visit to the nursery, we tell her how her infant will look and explain that a number of recent studies demonstrate that simply touching the infant after the acute period will help to relax him or her as well as to improve breathing, physical development, and rate of weight gain. Thus, the visit is important not only to the mother, but to the baby as well. Frequently a mother will say that she does not dare touch for fear that she will hurt or infect the baby. This may stem from her belief that she is an

inadequate or "bad" mother because she has not been able to produce a normal baby. It also has been, and still is, common for a
mother to have too much respect for the expert nurses and feel
inferior to them. It is beneficial for a mother to be aware of and to
express these feelings, but it is equally important for physicians and
nurses to convey acceptance of her concern and help her develop
self-confidence. By telling a mother, "Certainly you can come
in—the care you give the baby is special," health professionals are
essentially letting her know that they consider her a good person
and a wholesome, important influence on her baby.

The longer a mother must wait before she can see her baby,
the more time she has to imagine that her worst fantasies are true.
The sooner she sees her baby, the more rapidly she can reconcile
her image of him with his true physical condition. The first sight
and handling of the infant are never easy for the mother, who
brings to the experience her own set of worries and problems. She
should not be embarrassed or alarmed if she feels faint. The
mother who is able to face the difficulties of her small baby, to talk
about them, and to wrestle with her guilt feelings copes more
quickly and easily. Once these feelings are put into words, the family is on the road to becoming attached to the newborn.

A letter we received from a mother about her experience in
the premature nursery conveys vividly these early reactions:

> I felt angry when I would look up at a small group [doc-
> tors] standing next to me talking about my baby and not one
> would look at me. So I quit looking up, I quit expecting to
> be treated the same way one would in usual circumstances. I
> tried to learn the "rule." I was for the most part ignored. . . .
> I think I'm mad at the world. I'm mad at all the people who
> work in the premature nursery. Even the ones who aren't
> taking care of John. They're all in it together. They stole him
> from me. They have control over him. They tell me whether
> he's OK or not. They affect my well-being with the intona-

tion of their voices, their moods, their work load. . . . I can't tell you in this hostile environment with all these beeps and lights and where you have work responsibilities that I know will take you away in a few minutes. . . . I can't tell you in front of this little plastic bed where my baby is imprisoned, my baby who is such a mystery to me, who looks like a baby but whose insides don't seem to work right, and who may have had a serious mysterious bowel disease. . . . I can't tell you in this unsafe place that I'm afraid my baby will die, because it hurts too much and I don't want to feel it right now.

But I didn't have to say anything. She [a nurse] put her hand on my shoulder and said some small thing like, "It must be tough," and that was all she had to do. She acknowledged my feelings and helped a great deal in doing so.

THE INDIVIDUAL NEEDS OF EACH PREMATURE INFANT

During the many months of life in utero, the developing fetus is protected and buffered against harsh changes in the environment. Suspended in amniotic fluid, the fetus is also weightless. To reduce the disruptive effects of the nursery environment, the psychologist Heidi Als and others have developed a sensitive method of individualized care of the premature infant that takes into account what each infant is seen to experience as soothing or disruptive.[5] This detailed examination is done in the first days after birth and becomes the basis for each infant's specific care plan. Each infant's requirements for light, sound, position, and special nursing care are developed only after the detailed behavioral assessment. These individualized nursing-care plans for high-risk, low-birth-weight infants, involving their behavioral and environmental needs, make a remarkable difference in how well the infants recover.

In two randomized trials using this approach, infants receiving individualized behavioral management required many fewer days on a respirator and fewer days on supplemental oxygen. In addition, their average daily waking time increased, they were discharged many days earlier, and they had a lower incidence of intraventricular hemorrhage. Following discharge, their behavioral development progressed more normally and their parents were more able to develop ways of sensing their needs and responding and interacting with them pleasurably. Parents have an easier time adapting to premature infants who are more responsive. As the infant develops, the parents gain much by assisting with the observations and helping the nurse develop the care plan.

Sensory stimulation of healthy, physiologically stable infants also plays a role in neurological and physical maturation. If a small, premature infant is touched, rocked, fondled, cuddled, or talked to daily during her stay in the nursery, she may have fewer pauses in breathing and increased weight gain, and more rapid progress in some areas of higher brain functioning, which may persist for months after discharge from the hospital.[6]

Simply fondling the premature infant for five minutes out of every hour for two weeks alters bowel motility, crying, activity, and growth. Massage of preterm infants fifteen minutes three times a day also results in less stress behavior, superior performance on the Brazelton Neonatal Behavior Assessment scale, and, more importantly, better performance on a developmental assessment at eight months.[7]

As the staff of a premature nursery plans the care of an infant, the most difficult and important question is whether the stimulation is beneficial or harmful to the infant. The stimulation must be appropriate to each infant's state of development and individual requirements, since there is danger in overstimulation of the immature nervous system.

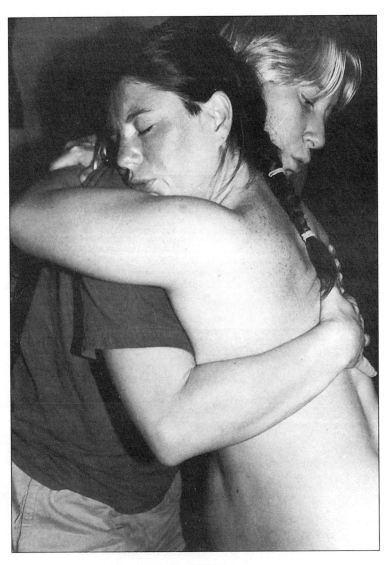

Illustration 1
A woman in labor needs total support–
in order to let go completely.
Patty Ramos

Illustration 2 After a long labor–the gift. *Leroy Dierker*

Illustration 3 In rapt, mutual gaze, the first dialogue begins.

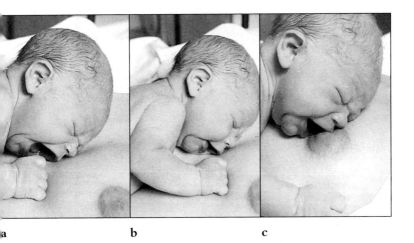

a   b   c

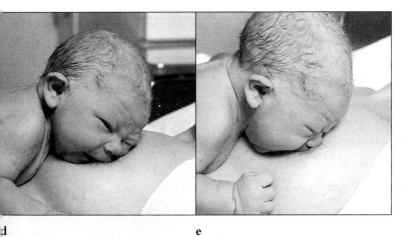

d   e

Illustration 4
Less than one hour old, this baby boy
crawls up his mother's body and
latches onto her breast, all by himself.
Lennart Righard

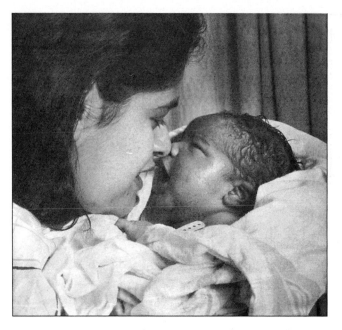

Illustration 5 A special intimacy often begins in the first hours of life. *Leroy Bierker*

Illustration 6 Twelve hours after birth, this father and baby are getting to know each other. *Suzanne Arms*

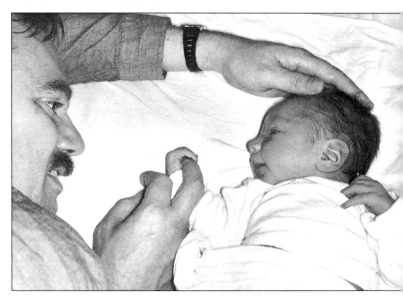

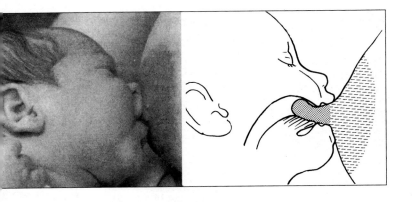

Illustration 7
This baby is sucking on the mother's nipple,
which frequently leads to problems or early weaning.
Below: In the "correct" position, the baby's lips
are on the areola and the nipple is far back
in the baby's mouth and not injured.
Lennart Righard

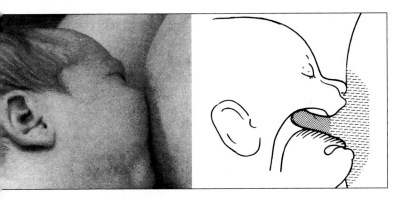

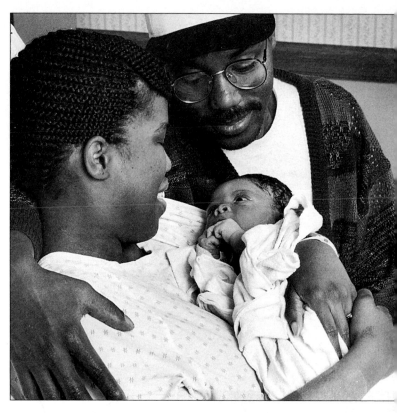

Illustration 8
In the postpartum period,
communication must be
three ways.
Leroy Dierker

Opposite

Illustration 9
A 1.2-pound premature baby,
skin-to-skin with her mother.
Jorge Martinez

Illustration 10 One month later.
Jorge Martinez

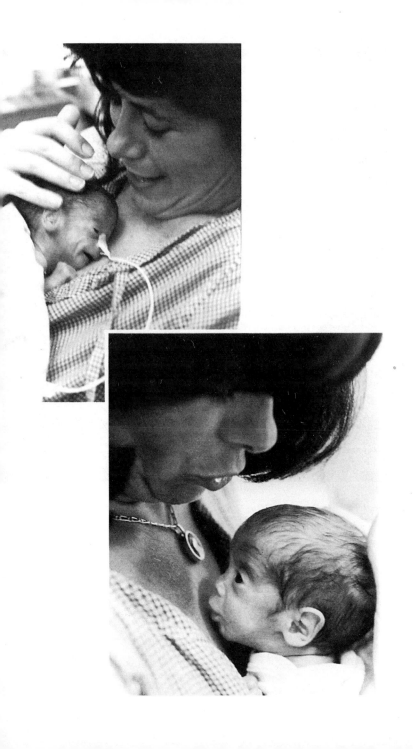

Illustration 11
A confident mother offers "kangaroo care"
in a corner of the intensive care unit to her
prematurely born (six and one-half-month) baby,
one month after birth.
Suzanne Arms

HOW PARENTS CAN BECOME INVOLVED

The degree to which a mother can care for her baby during the period in the intensive care nursery will obviously influence their relationship. We have been impressed with the ingenuity of nurses in developing techniques that allow a mother to hold her baby in her arms while the baby is being fed by nasogastric tube. They attach the burette to the mother's gown, which permits her to hold her baby until all the feeding has run into the infant's stomach. We have found notes tacked to the baby's bed: "Please hold my 1:00 feeding for my mother. She will come to give me my feeding. Boy, will I be glad to see her! Signed, Susie."

Studies of infant development have suggested that contingent stimulation (i.e., stimulation related to cues from the infant) may aid in any infant's development. Therefore, we suggest that, as much as possible, mothers fondle and talk to their babies as they would normally if the baby were not in the hospital.

The case of Benjamin, who weighed one pound, fifteen ounces at birth, is an example of the importance of such stimulation by one person consistently. Benjamin was extremely immature, was fragile in appearance, and had frequent breathing pauses, of which his mother was aware. After being informed of the importance of stimulation, his mother came to the hospital early each morning and stayed until noon, then returned after lunch and stayed until 6:00 P.M., when her husband finished his work. Her efforts with the baby were sensitively adjusted to him and consisted of considerable talking and stroking. Gradually she assumed more and more responsibility for his feeding and care. Benjamin's significant decrease in breathing pauses, unusually rapid weight gain, and developmental progress in the hospital as well as in subsequent months were remarkable. The staff repeatedly told the mother that Benjamin was doing extremely well "due to her efforts"—a sincere statement, since the baby's progress was noticeably better than expected. Both staff and mother recognized that she was making an important contribution when they saw that on several days the breathing pauses were frequent during the night but were almost absent when she was present. This mother was able to establish a reciprocal interaction with her baby. She could send messages to him by stroking and talking and could receive messages in return, such as a change in activity level or an opening of the eyes.

Several students of young premature infants, including Peter Gorski[8] and T. Berry Brazelton, have noted that when the visual attention of some infants is captured by an adult, they are so captivated by the experience that they can forget to breathe and often become blue. Until we have defined more closely the sensory needs and tolerances of premature infants, we must continually observe how the immature infant is managing exciting new experiences. Just as Als has adapted the environment of infants to meet their individual needs,[9] perhaps in the future we will be able to read the signals given to us by premature infants and thus to help them, in effect, to regulate their own environment. Several studies have identified promising possibilities for new approaches to care. In one study, premature infants in an isolette would move and spend more time in contact with a small "breathing" teddy bear in contrast to a teddy that did not make breathing movements.[10] Interestingly, eight weeks after leaving the hospital, the infants with breathing teddies spent a greater amount of each day in quiet sleep. The long-term effects of adapting the early environment of premature infants to their needs were dramatized when researchers in England turned the light out at night in a "growing nursery" for the last two weeks of hospital stay for one group of infants and left them on continuously for another group.[11] The two groups of infants appeared to be similar until five to six weeks after discharge. At that point, infants whose nursery had had day and night cycles for the two weeks of their hospital stay slept two hours longer per twenty-four hours and spent one hour less each day feeding. Three months after discharge, they were a pound heavier than infants who had not had the lights out at night.

THE EFFECTS OF PARENT INVOLVEMENT

Not long ago, parents were not even allowed in premature nurseries. The first study to investigate the feasibility of permitting parents into the premature nursery began at Stanford University, in California.[12] The researchers questioned whether parents of premature infants suffered from deprivation due to their long physical separation from their hospitalized infants. For two years they studied the practicality of allowing mothers (forty-four in all) into the nursery soon after birth, first to handle and then to feed their infants while they were still in incubators. Three groups of mothers from similar socioeconomic backgrounds were observed. One group of mothers was given contact with their premature infants in the intensive care unit in the first five days of life, a second group of mothers was separated from their premature infants with only visual contact for the first twenty-one days (the practice of the day), and a third group of mothers of full-term infants had routine contact with their infants at feedings during a three-day hospitalization. When the separated infants reached four and three-fourths pounds, at ages ranging from three to twelve weeks, they were transferred to a discharge nursery where their mothers were allowed to be with them as much as they desired for the seven to ten days until discharge at a weight of five and a half pounds. When the babies were able to be fed easily by nipple, the mothers were encouraged to breast-feed.

Originally, the threat of infection had been a formidable deterrent to permitting parents to enter the nursery. To evaluate this potential danger, cultures were taken weekly from the umbilicus, skin, and nostrils of each infant and from the nursery equipment, for the entire period that mothers were allowed into the unit. The results of these cultures showed no increase in potentially dangerous bacteria as a result of mothers' presence in the nursery. In fact, the number of positive cultures actually declined during the study. Investigators also observed that mothers washed more frequently and more thoroughly than both the nurses and house officers.

The interactions between the mothers of these three groups and their own infants were observed three times: just before discharge, a week later, and then a month after discharge. The mothers of full-term infants smiled at their babies more and had more complete contact with them. On the other hand, no striking differences were found between the behaviors of the separated and contact mothers of premature infants. However, the first-time mothers in the separated group showed significantly less self-confidence in their ability to care for their infants.

When mothers are first permitted to touch their premature babies, they typically begin by circling the incubator and touching the baby's extremities with the tips of their fingers. These reactions are different from those of the parents of full-term infants, who by the end of the first visit of the baby to the mother are stroking the infant's trunk with the palm of their hand. Mothers of full-term infants will also more frequently align their head with their babies' heads in the "en face" position.[13]

Interestingly, only one of twenty-two mothers in the contact group became divorced during the period of the study, whereas five of twenty-two mothers in the separated group were divorced.[14] It is worthy of note that a prerequisite for admission into the study was that the parents planned to keep and raise their babies. Nevertheless, in two cases in the separated group, the baby was given up for adoption because neither parent wanted custody.

In a study carried out in the University Hospital in Cleveland, fifty-three mothers of premature infants were assigned, on the basis of when the baby was born, to two groups, "early contact" and "late contact."[15] Mothers in the early contact group were allowed to come into the premature nursery to handle and care for their premature infants one to five days after birth. The late contact group of mothers was not permitted to enter the nursery until twenty-one days after birth. For the first three weeks these mothers had only visual contact with their infants through the nursery windows (not an unusual practice in the 1970s).

Time-lapse movies of both groups of mothers feeding their infants were taken just before discharge and one month later. The mothers who had early contact spent significantly more time looking at their infants during the first filmed feeding. There was a thought-provoking correlation between the amount of time mothers looked at their babies during the second filmed feeding and the infants' IQ scores on the Stanford-Binet test at forty-two months of age. That is, mothers who had early contact with their infants spent more time looking at them during feedings, and these children had significantly higher IQ scores—a mean of ninety-nine for early contact children compared with a mean of eighty-five for late contact children.

Neither group of investigators found it possible to run the early and late contact groups in the nursery simultaneously. Each study had a three-month period of late contact, followed by three months of early contact, to prevent late contact mothers from observing early contact mothers in the nursery. Eventually both studies were discontinued because they were too painful for the nurses, who had begun to feel that it was unfair not to permit all mothers to have early contact with their infants. These two studies paved the way for opening the doors of the premature nursery to parents.

Although parent visits in the intensive care nursery are now permitted and encouraged, studies continue to reveal that most parents of premature babies suffer severe emotional upheaval. In spite of this anxiety, parents believe that the opportunity to have contact with their infants in the neonatal intensive care unit is valuable.[16]

With the development of perinatal centers for high-risk infants, an increasing number of mothers have been transported to the maternity division of hospitals with an intensive care nursery before delivery. This enables them to visit and care for their infants during the early postpartum period, a trend that is helpful for both parents, since the father is not distracted by having members of his family in two hospitals. Infant mortality is significantly less when the mother is transported before giving birth, since facilities for early care of the high-risk infant are often more developed in a hospital with intensive care facilities. If there is not sufficient time to arrange for her transport before giving birth, we strongly recommend that the mother be moved during her early postpartum period. Nothing substitutes for the mother touching and holding her new infant. Doing so helps in the development of the mother's tie to her new infant and decreases some of her concerns.

As a result of observing premature nurseries in several countries over the years, we believe there should be no limit on parental visiting. Inflexible regulations isolate mothers and fathers from their infants, drastically increasing their anxiety about the baby's condition. Whether or not there is rooming-in, the nursery should be open for parental visiting twenty-four hours a day. Regulations regarding visits from others—grandparents, siblings (after discussion and preparation), other supportive relatives, and a friend of the mother, if the father is unavailable or unable to visit—should be flexible. Infections have not been shown to be a problem if proper precautions are taken, such as informing parents that they can enter only if they are feeling well, have no upper respiratory tract problems or other infectious diseases, and wash their hands thoroughly for four to five minutes before entering.

Parents of a premature infant need, besides ready access to their newborns, specific kinds of support and guidance from the staff. First, they need help in developing mutual interaction so that they will be attuned to the baby's special needs and can begin to feel close. They should be allowed and helped to care for their infant while still in the hospital so that after discharge they feel competent and more relaxed. Parents also need encouragement to work together during the crisis of the premature birth and to discuss any difficulties with one another about their abruptly changed circumstances.

ROOMING-IN

Early contact is further enhanced when mother and baby can share a room. A pioneering approach to helping parents adapt to a sick or premature infant was developed by pediatrician Donald Garrow at a district general hospital in High Wycombe, England.[17] The twenty-bed special infant care unit accommodates eight mothers at a time and 250 admissions each year. No matter how seriously ill they may be, some 70 percent of the babies have their mothers with them from the first few hours of life. Fathers may stay at night, and young siblings may visit as frequently as desired each day. Six of the mothers' rooms open directly into the infant special care unit so the parents can easily see or care for their infants. Infection has not resulted from allowing free entry to fathers, siblings, and grandparents. However, parents are told that children with diarrhea, fever, an upper respiratory tract infection, or any exposure to a contagious disease should stay home. Many mothers come to this special unit immediately after giving birth, and the nursery staff cares for both the mothers and the infants. Generally the mothers eat together, which allows time for them to share experiences and mutual support. When an infant death occurs, the mother involved usually remains on the unit for a day or so, and the nurses and one or two other mothers are often a great help to her in her grief.

When we visited the High Wycombe unit, the staff said that parents move more quickly to assume caregiving tasks, are less jealous of the staff and more chatty, and more readily adapt to the birth of a sick infant than previously, when mothers could not live in. The High Wycombe model has been closely watched and, in some cases followed in part by high risk nurseries in the United States.

In several countries throughout the world, including Argentina,[18] and Brazil, Chile,[19] South Africa,[20] Ethiopia,[21] and Estonia,[22] mothers of premature infants live in a room adjoining the premature nursery, or they room in. This arrangement appears to have multiple benefits. It allows the mother to continue producing milk, permits her to take on the care of the infant more easily, greatly reduces the caregiving time required of the staff for these infants, and allows a group of mothers of premature infants to talk over their situation and gain from discussion and mutual support.

We have studied what happens when mothers are permitted to live in with their infants before discharge, a practice we have termed "nesting." As soon as babies reached three and a half to four and a half pounds, each mother, in a private room with her baby, provided all caregiving. Impressive changes in the behavior of these women were observed. Even though the mothers had fed and cared for their infants in the intensive care nursery on many occasions before living in, eight of the first nine mothers were unable to sleep during the first twenty-four hours. Most of the mothers closed the door to the room, completely shutting out any chance of observation, often to the consternation of the nurses, who felt a strong responsibility for the infants' well-being. It was interesting to observe that the mothers rearranged the furniture, crib, and infant supplies. However, in the second twenty-four hour period the mothers' confidence and caregiving skills improved greatly. At this time, mothers began to make preparations at home for the baby's arrival. Several insisted on taking their infants home earlier than planned. The babies seemed to be quieter during this living-in period. In some mothers there were physical changes, such as increased breast swelling accompanied by some milk secretion. The mothers were not satisfied with the living-in nesting procedure until we established unlimited visiting privileges for the fathers and provided them with comfortable chairs and cots.

Initially we had difficulties in defining clearly the role of the nurse in the living-in or nesting unit. Unless the roles of the nurse and the mother are clarified, tussles will arise over who makes the decisions. We soon realized that the mother should be the responsible caregiver, and the nurse must function as a consultant.

KANGAROO CARE

The concept of kangaroo care started in Bogota, Colombia, as a solution for overcrowding in the premature nursery and a high death rate due to hospital-acquired infections. The Bogota nursery staff focused on educating and motivating the mother as the key person for the baby's survival, discharging the baby home as early as possible to minimize exposure to infection, encouraging bonding and exclusive breast-feeding, and keeping the baby warm by skin-to-skin contact inside the mother's clothes. The baby was held vertically between the mother's breasts to minimize problems of choking and aspirating.

There are still many questions about whether it is reasonable to care for tiny, low-birth-weight infants by this method in developing countries. However, carefully conducted studies have shown that stable infants weighing two pounds can be safely held skin-to-skin in a neonatal intensive care nursery such as those in the United States and other industrialized countries. The baby's body temperature is well maintained by the warmth of the mother's or father's skin when the baby wears a cap and is covered by a light blanket. The same studies have shown that the blood oxygen levels are higher and more favorable while the baby is skin-to-skin with the mother for periods of up to four hours a day. After a mother has had skin-to-skin contact with her tiny, fragile premature infant, starting soon after birth, it is perhaps not surprising that her confidence level in the nursery and when she goes home is greater than that among mothers without this experience (see Illustrations 9 and 10). At six months of age the babies who have had kangaroo care cry significantly less than babies without this care. With assurance about the safety and the benefits for both mother and baby, more nurseries are providing the kind of kangaroo care pictured in Illustration 11.

An increasing number of parents are requesting this experience. In South America, the United States, and Europe, mothers and fathers have found that holding the infant skin-to-skin is uniquely helpful as they develop a tie to their infant.[23] At the first skin-to-skin experience the mother is usually tense, so it is best for the nurse to stay with her to answer questions and make any necessary adjustments in position or to maintain warmth. A few mothers find that one such experience is enough for them. However, most mothers find the experience especially pleasurable. After the kangaroo contact some mothers have mentioned that they began for the first time to feel close to their baby and to feel that the baby was theirs. The photos on the three preceding pages show mothers and babies in various stages of development in skin-to-skin contact. Without prompting, one mother said that she was feeling much better because she was now doing something for her baby that no one else could do.

We view skin-to-skin care as a major advance in helping parents develop a closer tie to their infant. Detailed observations have been made of the infant's heart rate, temperature, and respiratory rate during kangaroo care. These remain stable, and pauses in breathing do not increase during the daily one- to one-and-a-half-hour experience. In addition, with kangaroo care, the mother's milk supply increases significantly, as does success in nursing.[24]

CARE OF PARENTS

In many neonatal intensive care units, groups of parents of premature infants meet together, once a week or more often, for discussions of their situation. Parents find both support and considerable relief from being able to express and compare their feelings. Parents who participated in such groups have been observed to visit their infants in the hospital significantly more often than those who do not participate.[25] They also talk to, and look at, and touch their infants in the en face position more and rate themselves as more competent on infant care measures. These mothers continue to show more involvement with their babies during feedings and are more concerned about their general development three months after their babies' discharge from the nursery.

The following unusual letter to one of the authors evokes the deep, intuitive support that one mother can give another:

[My baby] was born in the late evening after a fairly rapid labor and immediately whisked away to the intensive care unit. I was transferred to a side ward off the main postnatal ward. The next day I was lying there feeling very confused. It is strange after having this constant companion during pregnancy, and the anticipation of labor, to be suddenly left with nothing. I knew with my mind that she existed and would be returned to me, but my body didn't understand.

A woman came in to see me from the main ward. She was a friend and we knew each other well. She had had her baby two days before. She asked if I had had mine and I remember saying, "They tell me I have." She went away and brought her baby back, full of joy and pride, and thrust him into my arms.

Holding the baby, I had a startling and intense sensation of release. It really was as if some lock had been undone, and the tension could disappear, and I could understand the events of the previous day. I cuddled the baby for a few minutes and admired him and gave him back.

After that everything seemed normal. I believed in the existence of my baby and was able to wait for her peacefully.

I explained this to myself by thinking that some hormone had been released by the trigger of holding the baby. My body felt different afterwards, as if something necessary had happened, without which the normal postnatal events and changes could not take place. The experience was so strong that I have wondered ever since whether it might be necessary for every mother to hold and cuddle a baby, not necessarily her own, in the first day after birth. I don't think there would be any danger of bonding to another woman's baby, there was no feeling of that, only of allowing something to happen that would enable the bonding process to take place later, as appropriate.

MILESTONES

As the days progress and the small premature infant starts to grow, the mother begins to believe that her baby will most likely survive. As she starts caring for him, she readjusts her previous image of the imagined baby to one that is closer to the infant before her. It is remarkable to notice that mothers often comment on how much bigger the baby appears whenever there is any evidence of improvement—a slight weight gain, a feeding taken by nipple, or a decrease in the use of monitors or other support equipment. Most parents consider the removal of catheters or monitors, the onset of weight gain, and the change from feeding by tube to feeding by nipple to be major milestones in the development of the infant, whereas the staff takes them as routine. Progress, however, is not always straightforward, and if the infant loses a few grams of weight, parents will be alarmed, even though this occurs often in the premature nursery.

Many mothers have mentioned that they do not feel close to their babies until they actually have them in their arms during a feeding and do not feel really close until they are feeding their babies at home. The fishbowl effect of a glass-walled nursery is a barrier to their feelings of attachment. The more privacy they have, the warmer they feel toward their infants. If at all possible, small rooms should be provided for mothers so that they will have privacy while feeding and cuddling their infants.

One of the best indicators of the parents' progress is their visiting pattern. Is the number of visits decreasing or increasing? Is the mother beginning to consider the baby a member of her family? Are the parents starting to make plans at home for their infant—painting the room or buying new curtains and equipment they will need? Are they preparing the nest? The overly optimistic mother who appears unconcerned about her baby's progress, who does not ask any questions, and who is passive or indifferent is worrisome to the medical staff. We are concerned about the mother who denies. When parents appear extremely confident about their ability to care for their infant and rarely ask questions or listen to the nurses' suggestions, the road ahead could be unnecessarily rocky. Once these parents and their baby are at home, we are not surprised when they become unusually anxious and make many frantic telephone calls to the nursery. Parents who grapple with the problem from the start seem to get through the adjustments much better.

OVERCOMPENSATION

A problem sometimes observed in mothers of premature infants was observed in the following case from the authors' practice. While this case is somewhat extreme, the risk that it demonstrates of unresolved feelings surrounding prematurity is worth keeping in mind.

Claire, a three-year-old, was referred for consultation after she had been asked to leave several preschools because of her unpredictable behavior. She was having difficulty in controlling aggressive outbursts of anger and would suddenly lash out and hit other children. She had a very low tolerance level and always wanted what she desired immediately. At home Claire never seemed to have enough.

Claire was born prematurely, received surfactants and oxygen therapy for two days, and made satisfactory progress. She grew nicely on breast milk and was discharged home after four weeks. Her mother, Patty, first began to feel that Claire was "her baby" when she took her home and assumed all of her care. During the first year, Claire was an easy baby; however, her mother worried that her development would not be normal because of what she had read in books about premature infants. Patty noted that Claire did not seem very curious or interested in her and seemed more devoted to her father. She had the feeling that Claire was very needy and that she could "never do enough for her." Patty offered her food, toys, and many different objects even before she fussed. Patty recognized that she probably had done too much for Claire and did not let her figure things out for herself. She felt that Claire, rather than she, was in control much of the time.

After discussing all this at some length, Patty began to appreciate that she had purposely set no limits on Claire, wanting to make up to her for her premature birth. Patty also realized that her sense of being out of control eventually made her become very angry so that she disciplined Claire inconsistently. She was able to recognize how important it was for Claire to have limits and see that her worries about prematurity should not determine the way she raised her daughter.

In a later interview Patty also said that in the first year she had never been sure that she was bonded to her daughter, and she began to note that her overdoing for Claire was possibly an overcompensation because she was not sure that she felt close to Claire. After she appreciated that it was important to set boundaries, and understood the reasons why she might not have wanted to set boundaries, a remarkable improvement in Claire's behavior occurred both at home and in nursery school. Claire began to feel more secure and gradually learned new ways to handle her own anger.

Once Patty could free herself from this overcompensation, she was able to set limits for Claire without anxiety or fear of "depriving her." When Claire was racing around, banging and pulling things wildly, Patty lovingly but firmly acknowledged her feelings and told her that although she understood what she wanted to do, it was not okay at that time. Patty then helped Claire redirect her energy and attention to a more appropriate activity.

The more fragile and precarious a premature baby's beginning, the more likely it is that the parents will continue to see the child as vulnerable, and will find it difficult to set firm limits. While this need to overcompensate is common and understandable, an awareness of its pitfalls can help parents avoid the long-term effects just described.

GOING HOME

Over the years, premature infants have been discharged at increasingly earlier dates from the hospital. Investigators who have explored the early discharge of premature infants when they weighed about five and a half pounds found no harmful effects on the infants' physical health. However, no systematic observations have been made of maternal behavior and anxiety or of later infant development in these cases. Kathryn Barnard, a nurse and child development specialist, pointed out the immense stress on parents brought about by early discharge:[26]

> Early discharge is appropriate as long as the parents are given the support they need. When home, there should be some-one to talk to by phone about their questions and someone who can give them reassurance about the baby's condition and their parenting. Even though there are no apparent physical adverse effects of early discharge, the tremendous anxiety some parents experience when taking very young or relatively unstable babies home in terms of feeding, temper-ature, and respiratory status may have profoundly adverse effects on the parent–infant interaction and later develop-mental outcome.

Before a premature baby is sent home, parents should have had the opportunity to spend several hours providing full care, including the administration of any medications that will be continued at home. We believe that two or three days of round-the-clock care provided by the parents, the "nesting" arrangements described earlier in this chapter, ensure even better preparation. This procedure might be compared with learning to fly with a co-pilot before attempting a solo flight.

Once the family is at home, they and their caregivers should be alert to situations in which the mother feels inadequate or highly anxious. Frequent telephone calls and more than one visit to the emergency room at a strange hour with a completely normal infant are signals for help. If the mother appears in the emergency room more than once, or seems desperate in other ways, we believe in admitting the infant, and having the mother stay with the baby as she tries to solve her worries.

During follow-up examinations, we watch for signs of attachment and confidence. Does the mother stand close by during the exam, watch the handling, and soothe the baby when he cries, or does she appear detached and look around the office and concern herself with other matters? Signs that worry us are a loose, distant hold on the baby; a propped bottle, whether the baby is held in the mother's arms or not; and a failure to hold the bottle so that milk can flow out of the nipple. In contrast, at this time we usually see many signs of attachment such as eye-to-eye contact, close contact with the baby during the feeding, and fondling, kissing, stroking, and nuzzling.

Parents should keep in mind the support still available to them in the first days and weeks at home. We recommend that a mother and father meet with the pediatrician one month after the baby has been discharged, when the infant is gaining and well. At these times we ask the parents to review in detail the events around the birth and the early days of the infant's hospital course. It is surprising how differently the two parents may recall the early minutes and hours, how confused they may be about what went on, and how often their concerns are completely different from those of the nurses and physicians. Because this one-hour interview is never sufficient time to cover everything, we encourage the husband and wife to continue the discussion, in minute detail, between themselves and then to call a day later to discuss the interview with us.

In a series of creative studies done both in the hospital and the home during the first three months after birth, Klaus Minde[27] and his colleagues observed the interaction of thirty-two mothers and their low-birth-weight infants. Highly interacting mothers who visit and telephone the nursery more while the infants are hospitalized stimulate their infants more when at home. On the other hand, mothers who stimulate their infants little in the nursery also visit and telephone less frequently and stimulate them little at home.

Investigators in England have noted that many mothers of infants weighting three pounds or less go through three phases in the first six months after the baby's discharge from the hospital.[28] At first there is a "honeymoon" phase. Excitement prevails, and the parents are usually euphoric at the time of the first visit to the clinic seven to ten days after discharge. A period of exhaustion follows, when the euphoria has waned and the mother has many minor complaints about the management of the baby, particularly about feeding. The mother not only looks exhausted but is exhausted. The feeding problems are often genuine. This phase will last until the time when the baby begins to smile and respond, which can take anywhere from a few days to several weeks. Concerning these phases, the psychologist Tiffany Field has observed, "Our experience with parents of ICU graduates (premature newborns) is that when they most need outside supports, that is, after the honeymoon phase when the infant is difficult and the parents exhausted, they have the least support. Perhaps more of our resources should be invested in home visiting programs."[29]

SOCIALIZING WITH A PREMATURE BABY

In an essay entitled "The Mirror Role of Mother and Family in Child Development," D. W. Winnicott noted that what the baby observes in the caregiver's face in the early months helps him develop a concept of self.[30] Winnicott asked, "What does the baby see when he or she looks at the mother's face? I am suggesting that, ordinarily, what the baby sees is himself or herself. In other words the mother is looking at the baby and what she looks like is related to what she sees there. All this is too easily taken for granted. I am asking that this which is naturally done well by mothers who are caring for their babies shall not be taken for granted." At another point he wrote, "Many babies (premature or sick), however, do have a long experience of not getting back what they are giving. They look and they do not see themselves. There are consequences. First, their own creative capacity begins to atrophy, and in some way or other they look around for other ways of getting something of themselves back from the environment." He suggested that blind infants need to get themselves reflected through senses other than sight. The important implication of Winnicott's perceptive observations is that in the normal full-term mother–infant pairs he cared for, the mother was often following or "imitating" the infant.

These observations were later supported by infant researcher Colwyn Trevarthan, who used fast film techniques and detailed analysis to observe mothers and infants, and noted that mothers imitate their babies during spontaneous play.[31] He suggested that it is the mother's imitation of her infant's behavior, rather than the reverse, that sustains their interaction and communication. Detailed analysis of the periods when both are active reveals that the mother is studiously imitating the infant's expressions with a lag of between 0.1 and 0.2 second. Thus, the infant is setting the pace.

Tiffany Field noted that in spontaneous play a mother and

her normal full-term infant are each interacting about 70 percent of the time.[32] However, when the mother is asked to increase her attention-getting behavior, her activity increases to 80 percent of the time, and, strikingly, the infant's looking decreases to 50 percent (and the infant partially turns off). In contrast, when the mother is told to imitate the movements of the infant, she moves at a much slower pace and the infant's looking time increases.

When observing high-risk premature infants at home at three months of age, Field noted that in the spontaneous situation the mother is interacting up to 90 percent of the time, whereas the infant is looking only 30 percent of the time. If the same mother is told to use attention-getting gestures, her activity increases even above 90 percent of the time and the infant's gaze decreases further. If the mother's activities are slowed down by asking her to imitate the baby's facial expressions and movements, there is, as with full-term babies, a striking increase in the infant's looking. In other words, while parents want to make every effort to encourage increased responses from a premature infant, if their efforts are too vigorous, the effort may be counterproductive, causing the infant to respond less. This is a very natural predicament for the mother of a premature infant. She may be trying to follow the work of stimulation that she observed in the premature nursery; she may be unhappy with the infant's responses and attempt to increase them, or she may develop this increased activity as a result of some natural intuitive compensatory reactions.

One of the most interesting observations we have found about such stimulation is based on the work of a special nurse, Louise, in our own nursery. We have always found her to be unusually perceptive and sensitive in picking out which infants will have problems in their first or second year. When premature infants who are unresponsive are taken out of the incubator, she usually takes over their care. Then, with her handling over several days, we see the infants become bright, begin to look around, follow faces, and increase their activity. On close filming of Louise, we see little apparent activity. She holds the infant eight to ten inches from her face and seems to move imperceptibly. From our understanding of the concepts of imitation developed by Winnicott, Trevarthan, and Field, it would appear that Louise may intuitively be following very slightly behind the movements of the premature infant and allowing the infant to begin to find himself. It should be noted that once a person is a self-contained individual and has a well-integrated self, any imitation is an invasion of that individual's integrity. However, during the early months when infants' selves are incompletely formed, imitation of the infants' gestures appears to be a help in their finding themselves.

All these observations suggest that we should be careful about recommending increased stimulation at home for the premature infant. Instead, it would appear to be more appropriate to suggest that the mother attempt to move at her premature infant's pace. When the mother is more perceptive of the infant's needs, the infant shows real delight and the mother receives pleasure in intimate play with her infant. It is no fun for the mother and father when the baby "turns off" and away because of being overwhelmed. The pleasure of learning to communicate with a small premature infant is in some ways like learning to ride a bicycle for the first time. These pleasurable interchanges are building blocks for infants and help with their development.

Recent studies involving large numbers of premature infants have revealed that home visits by infant specialists have many valuable effects.[33] These home visits help the mothers and fathers perceive the often subtle cues and individual needs that a premature infant transmits when communication begins in the first weeks and months at home. Mothers and fathers who have had a chance to look at their infants with the assistance of an infant specialist have had an easier time with the infants, and the babies appear to develop a bit more smoothly and rapidly. These home visits also give the parents an opportunity to ask questions.

RECOMMENDATIONS

The following general recommendations for care of premature or sick babies represent guidelines for providing an environment that will enhance the development of a strong parent–infant bond. Parents can use them to understand what to ask for, and professionals may find them useful in evaluating their own institution.

1. *First hour.* When a premature infant weighing between four and five and a quarter pounds is born and appears to be doing well without grunting or respiratory difficulty and the physician is relaxed about the health of the infant, we have found it beneficial for the mother to have the baby placed in her bed for twenty to sixty minutes in the first hour of life, with a heat panel above them and a nurse nearby.

2. *Accommodations.* A mother and her infant ideally should be kept near each other, on the same floor, in the same hospital. When the long-term significance of early mother–infant contact is kept in mind, some flexibility with current restrictions and territorial traditions seems appropriate and can usually be arranged. Furthermore, a mother appears to develop a more appropriate attachment if she can have some privacy with her infant in a separate room close to, or connected to, the unit.

3. *Transport.* In our transport system, if the baby needs to be moved to a hospital with an intensive care unit, we have found it helpful to give the mother a chance to see and touch her infant, even if he has respiratory distress and is in an oxygen hood. The house officer or the attending physician stops in the mother's room with the transport incubator and encourages her, if she desires, to touch her baby and look at him at close range.

Any comment about the baby's strength and healthy features made at this time may be long remembered and appreciated. The infant must be pink and adequately ventilating before we take him to his mother. If he is gasping and blue, resuscitative measures are taken, and our transportation team stays in the hospital until we can be sure of a safe trip. Transporting the mother and baby together to the medical center that contains the intensive care nursery is occurring more frequently in many communities. This trend should be encouraged because of its immediate and long-term benefits.

4. *Father's participation.* In the event that the baby needs to be transported, we encourage the father to follow the transport team to our hospital so that he can see what is happening with his baby. We urge the father to use this period of time to get to know the nurses and physicians in the unit, to find out how his infant is being treated, and to talk with the physicians in a relaxed fashion about what they expect will happen with the baby and her treatment in the succeeding days. We allow him to come into the nursery (and often offer him a cup of coffee), and we explain in detail everything that is going on with his infant. We ask him to act as a link between us, his family members, and the hospital by carrying information back to his wife so that he can let her know how the baby is doing. We suggest that he take a Polaroid picture, even when the baby is on a respirator, so that he can show and describe in detail to his wife how the baby is being cared for. Mothers often tell us how valuable the pictures are for keeping some contact with their infants while being physically separated.

5. *Initial visit to the nursery.* A mother should be permitted into the premature nursery as soon as she is able to maneuver easily, since her baby will make better progress once she is able to visit. It is important for her to realize that she may become faint or dizzy when she takes her first look at her infant. However, a nurse can stay at her side during most of the visit to describe in detail the procedures and the equipment (such as the monitors for respiration and heart rate, the umbilical catheter, the infusion lines for

feeding, the incubator, and the ventilator and endotracheal tube) being used.

6. *Cesarean birth.* We have found that most mothers who have had a cesarean delivery feel exhausted if they visit more than once a day after they are discharged from the hospital. For these mothers the single visit a day can be extended, but it is best that it not last more than a few hours in the first week.

7. *Family visits.* We encourage grandparents, brothers and sisters, and other relatives to view the infant through the glass window of the nursery so that they will begin to feel attached to her. We let grandparents and other close relatives and friends enter and touch the infant, if the parents wish. If the father is not available, we invite the mother to share the visits in the nursery with her mother or another relative or close friend.

8. *Discussions with parents.* At least once a day we discuss with the parents how the baby is doing. If the infant is critically ill, we talk with them at least twice a day. It is helpful if the mother tells the physician what she believes is going to happen or what she has read about the problem. Conversely, health professionals need to be sensitive to each mother's needs and to move at her pace during these discussions, to ensure that she understands everything that is said.

9. *Telephone communications.* While the physician is discussing the infant's condition by telephone with the mother, it is helpful if the father can get on another line so that he can hear the same words. This group communication reduces misunderstandings and usually is helpful in assuring both that they are hearing the whole story.

Parents are encouraged to call our unit at any time, day or night. This permits them to get an immediate report of their baby's status, activity, and color. This practice has occasionally led to confusion, because several nurses may report the same infant's condition within several hours and use slightly different words. Ideally, only one nurse should talk with the parents. However, this is not always practical, since shifts last only eight hours, and parents should be sensitive to these unavoidable differences. Usually the baby has one nurse with overall responsibility for primary care and then a designated primary nurse for each shift. The day secretary has the daily weights of the infants available at her desk and so can quickly report this information to the mother who calls and is waiting to speak to the nurse.

10. *Touching.* When the immature infant has passed the acute phase, both the father and the mother should touch and gently massage their infant. This helps the parents get to know him, reduces the number of breathing pauses (if this is a problem), increases weight gain, and hastens the infant's discharge from the unit. (Initially, if the infant is acutely ill, touching and fondling the baby sometimes results in a drop in blood level of oxygen; therefore, touching by the parents should begin when the infant is stable and the nurse or physician is agreeable.)

11. *Feedback from the infant.* We believe that the mother and father must receive feedback from their baby in response to their caregiving for them to develop a close attachment. If the infant looks at their eyes, moves in response to them, quiets down, or shows any behavior in response to their efforts, this will encourage the parents' feeling of attachment. Practically speaking, this means that the mother must catch the baby's glance and be able to note that some maneuver on her part, such as picking up or making soothing sounds, actually triggers a response or quiets the baby. We suggest to parents, therefore, that they think in terms of trying to send a message to the baby and of picking one up from him in return. Usually when we say this to the parents, they laugh; they think we are joking. We then explain that small premature infants do see and are especially interested in patterned objects, that they can hear as well as adults, and that evidence suggests they will benefit greatly from receiving messages.

Because the baby often sleeps for two or three hours, waking up for only a short time, the parents often need to stay in the nursery for long stretches to be able to catch one of these short periods. This may also require special help from the nurse or other caregiver. However, the effort is worth it, since feelings of love for the baby are often elicited through eye-to-eye contact.

12. *Kangaroo care.* Skin-to-skin care by the mother as she holds the baby on her bare chest is often very rewarding. Positioning, support, and encouragement by the baby's nurse are needed, just as at the mother's first visit to the nursery. The mother often begins to feel especially warm feelings toward her infant during these periods, and breast milk output increases significantly.

13. *Breast-feeding.* It is especially helpful for the mother to make some tangible contribution to her infant, such as providing breast milk. Breast milk may reduce the number of infections and other complications that the infant may encounter both in the nursery and after discharge. We suggest to all obstetricians referring patients that they enthusiastically recommend that the mother supply some of her own milk to meet her infant's nutritional needs. Many mothers of premature infants had not planned to breast-feed and may encounter some difficulty. However, even a small amount of milk production can represent an important contribution. On the other hand, a mother should not feel a great deal of disappointment if she is unable to provide sufficient milk for her baby or wishes to stop for other reasons.

The mother-to-mother support provided informally by a friend or by a member of an organized group such as the La Leche League has been extremely helpful for some mothers of premature infants with regard to breast-feeding. For any persistent problem with breast-feeding, a mother should make an appointment with a lactation consultant. (For further discussion of breast-feeding, see Chapter 5.)

14. *Nurse—mother interaction.* When first handling their babies, mothers should look to nurses for guidance, support, and encouragement. The nurses' guidance in how to hold, dress, and feed infants can be extremely valuable. Often mothers need special reassurance and permission before they can enjoy caring for their babies. In a sense, the nurse assumes the role of the mother's own mother, teaching her the basic techniques of mothering.

8

BIRTH DEFECTS
AND BONDING

When a baby is born with a malformation, it is a crushing blow to everyone who shares in the event. To the parents, for whom the newborn represents the culmination of their best efforts and embodies their hopes for the future, falls a burden of grief and adjustment and the need to learn new ways of caring. The birth of an infant with a congenital malformation also presents complex challenges to the caregiver who will care for the affected child and family.

Parental reactions are turbulent, and the usual pathways for the development of close parent–infant bonds are disrupted. The situation was well summed up by Bruno Bettelheim:

Children can learn to live with a disability. But they cannot live well without the conviction that their parents find them utterably lovable. . . . If the parents, knowing about his [the child's] defect, love him now, he can believe that others will love him in the future. With this conviction, he can live well today and have faith about the years to come.[1]

During a normal pregnancy, both mother and father develop a mental picture of their baby. Although the degree of concreteness varies, each has an idea about the sex, complexion, coloring, and so forth. As we have seen, one early task of parenting is to resolve the discrepancy between this idealized image of the infant and the actual appearance of the infant. The dreamed-about baby is a composite of impressions and desires derived from the parents' own experiences. If the parents have different cultural backgrounds, the tasks of reconciling the image to the reality is more complicated. However, the discrepancy is even greater if the baby is born with a malformation, and the parents must struggle to make the necessary major adjustment.

The reactions of the parents and the degree of their future attachment difficulties depend in part on the nature of the malformation:

Is it completely correctable or is it noncorrectable?
Is it visible or nonvisible?
Does it affect the central nervous system?
Is it life-threatening?
Will it affect the future development of the child?
Does it affect the genitalia? The eyes?
Is it a single or a multiple malformation?
Is it familial?
Will repeated hospitalizations and visits to physicians or
   agencies be needed?

INITIAL REACTIONS

The more visible the defects, the more immediate the result-ing concern and embarrassment. Even a minor abnormality of the head and neck results in greater anxiety about future development than an impairment of another part of the body.[2] This is also true for disabled adults with visible impairments, who experience more disruption in their interpersonal relationships than do those with nonvisible impairments.

Some parents feel reluctant to see their malformed babies at first and express a need to temper the intensity of the experience. When these parents do see their babies, it seems to mark a turning point, and caregiving feelings are elicited where previously there had been none. Parents often report that when they saw their infants for the first time, the malformations seemed less alarming than they had imagined. Seeing the children allayed some of their anxiety. In our own studies one parent reported, "We had been conjuring up all kinds of things—that there could be something wrong with every organ. But then what I saw was a relatively normal baby." Others report similar parental reactions—the information that something was wrong with the baby was often far more disturbing than the sight of the child. Mothers found that the time spent waiting to see the baby after being told about a congenital anom-aly was the most difficult to endure. Both the mothers and fathers were greatly relieved when they actually saw their children.

Ethel Roskies has written about the mothers of children with malformation caused by thalidomide.[3] She describes four mothers who were debating whether or not to institutionalize their children. The issue was settled when they saw their infants and found aspects they could "cherish." "When one mother looked into her baby's eyes he seemed to plead not to be aban-doned." In our studies the parents of children with visible problems had a shorter period of shock and disbelief than did the parents of a child with a hidden defect. The shock of producing a baby with a visible defect is stunning and overwhelming, but attachment can be facilitated by showing parents their newborn baby as soon as possible.

When 194 mothers of babies with spina bifida were interviewed, two-thirds of the mothers preferred to be told about the diagnosis as early as possible and were satisfied with the information they had received about the defects.[4] Any delay tended to heighten their anxiety. They objected to being given an unnecessarily gloomy picture at first. On the other hand, they also objected to having the seriousness of the condition minimized at first and aggrandized later. For example, one mother of an infant with a severe form of spina bifida called myelomeningocele was told that the baby had "just a small pimple on her back, but that was nothing for her to worry about." In our experience parents attach great importance to the approach and attitude of the medical and nursing staff. Although they often do not recall the exact words of the nurse, obstetrician, or pediatrician, they do remember their general attitude. Mothers who were hurt by an apparent lack of sympathy tended to attribute the abruptness to a lack of feeling in the informant, rather than to the likely cause—the difficulty of imparting such painful information. However, most mothers were impressed by the gentleness and sympathy extended to them by the nursing and medical staff. Small acts of kindness were clearly remembered years after the event.

A mother whom we once had in our practice, who had given birth to a daughter with Down syndrome, gave us an eloquent expression of her first reactions. She and her husband had their baby girl with them for many hours before her physician discussed his concerns with them. "Every mother in pregnancy must think, 'I want a healthy baby,' and you do have thoughts of having a baby with a problem. But the thought of mental retardation never entered my mind. When I thought about a problem with my baby, it was always something physical. When she was born and I looked at her, she was all in one piece and had ten fingers and ten toes. I thought, 'She's fine.' When they brought her to us and we looked at her, she looked physically fine. Of course, we never thought anything more than we had a girl with a fat neck. But it really gave us a chance to look her over, and we really studied her, turned her over, just looked at her, loved her, and we were already building that love."

To have had such a good beginning with their baby was important. It allowed the parents to complete the process of pregnancy and birth. The mother had delivered a "real" baby with identifiable characteristics to whom she could direct her active "mothering" impulses. Thus, when she received bad news about her baby, she was well under way with bonding to the baby and so did not have to initiate loving responses at the same time she was struggling with rejecting responses. She had been active in mothering already, and this was useful in coping with her mixed feelings. There is considerable debate about whether it is better to tell families that their baby has Down syndrome right away or whether to wait for several hours. We have no firm data, but based on our own experience, we believe it is desirable at least to take some time to be sure about our diagnosis and perhaps to allow the parents to spend a little time with the baby before we give them the news.

STAGES OF ADJUSTMENT

Despite the wide variations among the children's malformations and parental backgrounds, our studies have shown a number of surprisingly similar themes emerging from parental discussion of reactions.[5] Generally parents can recall the events surrounding the birth and their reactions in great detail. They go through similar identifiable stages of emotional reactions. Although the amount of time that a parent needs to deal with the issues of a specific stage varies, a sequence of stages reflects the natural course of most parents' reactions to their malformed infant.

First Stage: Shock

Most parents' initial response to the news of their child's abnormality is overwhelming shock. Parents report reactions and sensations indicating an abrupt disruption of their usual states of feeling. One mother said, "It was a big blow which just shattered me." One of the fathers explained, "It was as if the world had come to an end." Many parents confide that this early period is a time of irrational behavior, characterized by crying, feelings of helplessness, and occasionally an urge to flee.

Second Stage: Disbelief (Denial)

Many parents try either to avoid admitting that their child has a problem or to cushion the tremendous blow. They may wish either to be free from the situation or to deny its impact. One father graphically described his disbelief: "I found myself repeating 'It's not real' over and over again." Other parents mention that the news of the baby's birth did not make sense. One man admitted, "I just couldn't believe it was happening to me." Although almost every parent reported disbelief, the intensity of the denial varies considerably.

Third Stage: Sadness, Anger, and Anxiety

Intense feelings of sadness and anger accompany and follow the stage of disbelief. The most common emotional reaction is sadness. One mother reported, "I felt terrible. I couldn't stop crying. Even after a long while I cried about it." A smaller but significant number of parents report angry feelings. One father said, "I just wanted to kick someone." A mother reported that she was angry and "hated him [the baby] or hated myself. I was responsible." In most instances mothers fear for their babies' lives, despite strong reassurances. One mother said that she initially perceived her child as "nonhuman." "Holding him with that tube distressed me. Initially I held him only because it was the maternal thing to do." Almost all mothers of children with a malformation are hesitant about becoming attached to their babies.

Fourth Stage: Equilibrium

Parents then report a gradual lessening of both their anxiety and their intense emotional reactions. As their feelings of emotional upset lessen, they note increased comfort with their situation and confidence in their ability to care for the baby. Some parents reach this state of equilibrium within a few weeks after the birth, whereas others take many months. Even at best, this adaptation continues to be incomplete. One parent reported, "Tears come even yet, years after the baby's birth."

Fifth Stage: Reorganization

During this period parents deal with responsibility for their children's problems. Some mothers report that they had to reassure themselves that "the baby's problems were nothing I had done." Positive long-term acceptance of the child involves the parents' mutual support throughout the time after birth. Many couples have reported that they relied heavily on one another during the early period. However, in some instances the crisis of the birth separates parents. Some parents blame each other for the baby's birth. A mother may withdraw from her husband. "I don't want to see anybody. I just want to be by myself."

Despite these important similarities in parental reactions to various malformations, parents progress through the various stages of reaction differently. Some parents do not report initial reactions of shock and emotional upset but tend instead to intellectualize the baby's problem and focus on the facts related to the baby's condition. Other parents, unable to cope successfully with their strong emotional reactions to the birth, cannot achieve an adequate adaptation; they remain in a state of sorrow long after the birth.[6]

A recent study by pediatrician Jack Shonkoff and others showed that fathers and mothers had differing patterns of stress. Fathers noted greater stress associated with their feelings of attachment to their infants, while mothers reported more stress associated with the caretaking aspects of parenting.[7]

A lack of opportunity to discuss the infant's diagnosis can create a situation in which parents feel overwhelmed and unable to gauge the reality of their child's abnormality. If the mourning process becomes fixed as a sustained atmosphere within the family, the ghost of the desired, expected, healthy child sometimes continues to interfere with the family's adaptation to the real child. These findings confirm the work of psychoanalysts Albert Solnit and Mary Stark,[8] which has become the foundation of most therapeutic approaches to the parents of the malformed infant. Their analysis consists of the following elements:

1. The infant is a complete distortion of the dreamed-of or planned-for infant.
2. The parents must mourn the loss of this infant—a process that may take several months—before they can become fully attached to the living infant.
3. Along with this process of mourning there is a large component of guilt that takes many forms (such as the "mother's dedication of herself unremittingly and exclusively" to the welfare of the child while excluding others in the family) and requires great patience of the individual helping the family, since the parents may repeat the same questions and problems many times.
4. There is resentment and anger, which nurses, pediatricians, and obstetricians must often cope with, since it is sometimes directed toward them.

5. Parents should have the opportunity to express their own feelings and take whatever time necessary to experience the full extent of their grief.

6. The mother's attempts to withdraw her strong feelings from the expected perfect baby are disrupted by the demands of the newly arrived, imperfect child. The task of becoming attached to the malformed child and providing for his ongoing physical care can be overwhelming to parents at the time around birth, when they are physiologically and psychologically depleted.

7. The mourning cannot be as effective when the damaged child survives. The daily impact of this child on the mother is unrelenting and makes heavy demands on her time and energy.

Given the stress that is an inevitable part of these situations, it is remarkable that families who must cope with the intense emotional experience engendered by the birth of a malformed infant can learn to assimilate this child into the family and begin responding to the child's needs as readily as they do. As with other crises, success often strengthens people's ability to cope in other areas. The father of a boy with a congenital amputation described his confidence and pride in his management of the especially difficult time around his son's birth, his securing of treatment facilities, and his overall management of life. "I suppose you never know until you are all finished whether you have given your family what they need, but I try and I think I do a good job." Because parents and their disabled child face many problems in encounters with those outside the family, they develop special interactional skills in dealing with occurrences that other people might find embarrassing and distressing in the course of daily life with their child.[9] Parents of the disabled learn how to treat these events routinely. These special qualities, which may be characterized as "understanding" and "self-sacrifice," provide a rationale for the "deep philosophy" that persons with a stigma are said to evolve. The parents' identity, so compromised by the birth, may go through changes that result in a more positive self-image, although this kind of psychological maturity may evolve slowly.[10]

Struggling with these complex issues involves many tasks that can prevent lingering problems. For instance, parents, because of unresolved guilt and anger, may develop an overprotective attitude toward the child, which can thwart his development. Managing disturbed feelings by denying painful facts about a malformation can also lead to less than adequate resolutions. Other members of the family may be neglected if parents ward off the grieving process by establishing a guilty attachment to the child. If the mourning process is protracted, rather than diminishing, or if it develops into self-reproachful depression, the parent will not be able to contribute actively to the family.[11]

Responding to the birth of an abnormal child is exceedingly difficult because of the ambiguities involved. For example, what is the difference between overprotectiveness and responding to special needs? "It is hard, sometimes," said one mother, "to figure out what is being motherly and what is taking over. I want to help him as much as he wants and needs, but I don't want to hold onto him."[12] Realistically, it is true that the physical care required by such children is much greater than that required by normal children. Recurring hospitalizations for some, and uncertain developmental predictions for others, intensify parental concern and often frustrate consistent planning so that it is difficult to determine when parents cross the boundary into overprotective behavior.

Another feature to consider is the notion of just what characteristics constitute a good adaptation. If sorrow, depression, and anger are natural responses to the birth, and if the infant evoking these feelings continues to live, what is the right balance between mourning and acceptance? Researcher S. Olshansky coined the term "chronic sorrow" to describe some of the enduring aspects of parental reactions in adapting to a retarded child.[13] Chronic sorrow at some level may be constantly pres-ent in parents, especially if the child will always be dependent on them, as in some cases of retardation. Expecting the disappearance of the painful impact of this child on a family, under the guise that these feelings must be "resolved," can only force parents to deny their real feelings to professionals who may be able to help.

As many parents wrestle with these issues and search for some explanation of why this happened to them, they often experience concern over the exact cause of the problem—an issue that can be frustrating if a cause cannot be determined. When there is no acceptable medical explanation for the child's birth defect, the parents' genetic competence is called into question. They may try very hard to find a specific nongenetic cause for the problem in order to rid themselves of guilty feelings. Parents of children who develop mental retardation as a result of an illness such as meningitis subsequent to birth seem to adjust much better than parents with a baby retarded from birth.

An analysis of the anguished reactions of parents assuming new roles of parenting a handicapped child illustrates some typical responses. For example, the parents' search for causes sometimes leads to "doctor shopping," not because of dissatisfaction with the physician's diagnostic abilities, but because of the parents' need to alleviate their own guilt. Furthermore, the "active" search for services is often necessary because of the fragmentation of treatment facilities—one aspect of this crisis that parents are powerless to reverse.

It is disturbing when parents encounter a discrepancy between their own intense emotional turmoil and what they perceive as a lack of feeling on the part of professionals. A physician's objective professional manner may sometimes be mistaken for a lack of sympathy and may be met by generalized outrage on the part of the parents. Many physicians are able to find a balance between maintaining their own standards of correct professional behavior and at the same time fulfilling some of the parents' needs for support. For example, a physician can present the baby to the parents by focusing on normal features and positive attributes. As Albert Solnit has commented: "This focus can be helpful provided it is not used by physicians and nurses to 'turn off' the fears, questions, and resentment that many parents need to express before they can see and hear what the health personnel are presenting."[14] When parents are involved in the care and planning for their infant, they can enjoy satisfying feedback from him. At this early stage the groundwork is also laid for an effective alliance between parents and professionals concerning treatment. Nurses and physicians can help parents become attached to their malformed infant in the neonatal period and as the child grows.

In addition to their own emotional turmoil, parents must cope with the demands and expectations of those around them. With their ability to produce a normal child called into question and their emotional reserve at a low, they must face grandparents, friends, and neighbors. In this case, society has few of the built-in supports that are available in other crises such as the death of a relative or a community disaster. For example, friends and relatives send gifts and cards to the hospital after the birth of a normal baby, but, confused about the proper procedure when the baby is abnormal, they may find it easiest to forget to call or send anything. Parents are often reluctant to send out announcements of the birth or even to name the baby. As a result, they are likely to experience intense loneliness during the period immediately following the birth.

As we said before, the crisis of the malformed baby's birth has the potential for bringing the parents closer as a result of the mutual support and the communication required for adaptation. On the other hand, in many of the families we have studied, the baby's birth and the ongoing demands of the baby's care can create isolation between some parents, particularly if they do not share the responsibility. We have used the term *asynchronous* to describe parents who progress through the different stages of adaptation at different speeds. These parents usually do not share their feelings with each other and seem to develop difficulty in their relationships. Asynchrony often results in a temporary emotional separation of the parents and appears to be a significant factor in the high divorce rate after a major family crisis. A pediatrician who is sensitive to the relationship between parents is in a position to help with the family's adaptation by determining which stage of adaptation each parent has reached, and by making sure each partner is aware of the other's progress. Parents often speak of the importance of identifying the normal features of their child, which become increasingly evident as he grows. An alert pediatrician has an excellent opportunity to nurture this.

Finally, many parents say that the most effective way they have found to deal with the challenge is to take things day by day. They try not to worry excessively about the uncertainties in the future or to dwell on the traumatic events of the past. Sometimes this can be mistaken for defensive denial. Unless the daily care and planning for the child are affected, however, this type of reaction seems to protect parents from unbearable pain.

"Every day became a little bit easier," said one mother, "although now we know that there are going to be a lot of hard times to come." She went on: "I was having a very good day, this particular day, and Dick [her husband] walked in from his office. And whether he looked at me and knew I could finally handle his coming down or whether he had a bad day that day, I would say it was the first day that Dick was really way down. Then that Friday it was nice that a couple came to see us, because it brought him back up, and we both felt good." This couple have an intuitive grasp of each other's needs and strengths. For other couples, it may be more difficult to be reciprocal, to understand each other's place in the grieving process.

How parents change following the birth of a malformed infant is in part described by one father: "You never know how long each child is with you. You should take each one of them for every day you have them with you. And I think that has made us do a little bit more with our boy, Joshua.

"I think you grow out of it a little bit, but initially you are very vulnerable. This is so devastating that you almost expect something initially. You guard your other child very closely. At least I find myself doing that. So, I think you lose some of that vulnerability as you go on and get more comfortable with it." In these remarks the father displays remarkable sensitivity to the impact of this child on the whole family.

Commenting on parental adjustment to a malformed newborn, the pediatrician Morris Green has said, "It is almost as if birth becomes conception: A new image of this baby must gestate in the minds of parents." Throughout the various stages of this process there is, stresses Green, a need for competent, kind and supportive professional care, as well as mutual support and understanding between parents.[15] Effective communication between all of those involved in the care of the child is especially important. Above all, he emphasizes the importance of continuity in caring for these newborns after discharge, with regularly scheduled home and office visits. From the involvement of physician, nurse, parent educator, and parents there can grow an alliance that will work in the best interests of the child and the family.

RECOMMENDATIONS

1. *Initial contact.* We consider it a high priority for parents to see a baby born with a malformation as soon as possible so that both parents can observe his normal features as well as his abnormality. Any period of delay during which the parents suspect or know that their baby may have a problem but are unable to see him heightens their anxiety and allows their imaginations to run wild. They may jump to the conclusion that the baby is dead or dying while he is actually doing well and the problem is a cleft lip. The longer the period before they see the baby, the more distorted and fixed their concept of the baby's condition may become.

2. *Positive emphasis.* When first seeing the infant with a visible problem, it is important for parents to note all the normal parts as well and to recognize positive features such as his strength, activity, and alertness. It is sometimes surprising that malformations that appear obvious, striking, and bizarre to the physician sometimes do not seem to the parents frightening or disfiguring.

3. *Avoiding tranquilizers.* We have strong reservations about the use of tranquilizing drugs for the parents of a baby with a congenital malformation. Tranquilizers tend to blunt their responses and slow their adaptation to the problem. However, a small dose of a short-acting sedative at bedtime for sleeping is often helpful.

4. *Special caregiving.* Most maternity units are designed for the care of healthy mothers and babies. Therefore, when a baby is born with a problem such as a congenital malformation, the mother's mood and needs are out of step with the routines of the floor. Usually there is no special provision to meet the needs of the small group of parents with babies with malformations. They suffer from the assembly-line routines set up to provide care for the large volume of parents with husky and fully intact newborns. Physicians and nurses may cheerfully burst into the room and ask how the baby is doing, forgetting that he has been kept in the nursery because of the problem or has been transferred to another hospital or division. We try to assign a specific nurse to the mother of such an infant. This nurse needs to have the ability to sit for long periods with the mother and just listen to her cry and tell about her powerful reactions, which are often disturbingly critical and negative.

5. *Prolonged contact.* We believe that it is best for an infant to be with his or her mother for the first few days rather than being rushed to another division or hospital where special surgery will eventually be done. Obviously, if surgery is required immediately, this must be done without delay, but even in these cases it is desirable and usually safe to bring the baby to the mother and show her how normal the baby is in all other respects and to let her touch and handle her baby if at all possible. The father should be included in all discussions and in all periods of contact with the baby. We try to arrange for the mother and father to have extended periods with their infant to become acquainted with all the baby's features, both positive and negative. The mother of a normal infant goes through a period of one to three days in which she gradually realigns the image in her mind of the baby she expected with the image of the actual baby she delivered. When the baby has a malformation, the task of realigning the images is more difficult, and the result is a greater need for prolonged mother–infant contact. Investigators have noted significantly greater visiting if an infant with an abnormality has been home for a short while before surgery was required.[16] In those cases when the baby had been home two weeks or more, 65 percent of the newborns were visited on 90 percent to 100 percent of the days of hospitalization. For those newborns who were home for less than two weeks, the statistics fell off dramatically. Not more than 20 percent to 25 percent were visited with the same frequency.

6. *Visiting.* We encourage the extension of visiting hours in the maternity unit to allow fathers of malformed infants to spend prolonged periods with their wives. In this way they can share their feelings and start working through their sequence of reactions as synchronously as possible. Our hospital policy permits fathers to live-in with the mother and stay overnight.

7. *Questions.* Parents who are making a reasonably good adaptation often ask many questions and at times appear over-involved in the details of clinical care. Although these parents may be bothersome at times, we are usually pleased when we see this behavior. We are more concerned about parents who ask only a few questions and who appear stunned and overwhelmed by the infant's problem.

8. *Adaptation.* The process of adaptation to a malformation requires a long time before the parents are able to take care of the infant easily. During the early phases, when they are mourning the loss of the perfect baby they had anticipated, they may be unable to manage rather simple procedures. For example, tube feedings that can be managed easily at two to three months sometimes cannot be handled by fairly adept parents in the first few days or weeks.

9. *Understanding findings.* Parents should realize that many problems of malformed or sick babies are highly frustrating, not only to themselves but to the physicians and nurses as well. When things are not going well, the physicians and nurses may go through some of the same reactions—feeling defeat, sadness, anger, and anticipatory grief—as the parents. The many questions asked by a parent who is trying to cope with the problem and understand it can be frustrating for the physician, especially if the parent asks the same questions over and over again during the first three to four months. The psychological reaction of denial is sometimes so strong that the parents may insist they have never heard about the kidney problem, the mental retardation, or the possibility that the problem might be genetic, even though these may have been discussed on several occasions for at least an hour. It takes time to integrate this information.

10. *Possible retardation.* If there is a chance of the infant being retarded, we strongly believe that physicians should not discuss it with the parent unless they know with almost absolute certainty that the infant is damaged. This controversial recommendation stems from the many cases in which excellent physicians expressed this suspicion, but later found that this was incorrect and then discovered that they could not convince the parents that the child was normal, even years later. Many of these youngsters have subsequently experienced major developmental disturbances because their parents continued to treat them as if they were retarded. It is also extremely difficult to make predictions about such babies in the first few weeks of life. In the high-risk nursery attended by one of the authors, we found that expert neonatologists and neurologists, using all the common medical procedures, made correct predictions of normality or abnormality in complicated high-risk infants only 50 percent of the time.

11. *Progressing at the parents' pace.* It is generally difficult for parents to absorb information about several major problems in their baby all at the same time. We try to move at the parents' pace and, where necessary, show them one problem at a time. If physicians move too rapidly, parents tend to retreat, unable to take in all the medical material.

12. *Discussions with physicians.* The series of reactions to the birth of a baby with a malformation are such that each parent may move through the stages of shock, denial, anger, guilt, sadness, adaptation, and reorganization at a different pace. If they are unable to talk with each other about their reactions and feelings concerning the baby, a severe disruption in their own relationship may develop. Therefore, we recommend that parents have several private meetings with physicians to explore how the mother is doing, how she feels her husband is managing, how he feels about the infant, how he is coping, and how he thinks his wife is managing. In this way parents can start to think not only about each other but about their own adaptation. Often communication between the parents improves after one or two of these sessions.

13. *Communication between the parents.* If the parents are communicating reasonably well, we often urge them to spend some time alone together after supper and go over how they have really felt hour by hour from the time of the baby's birth, to talk about their own feelings and impressions no matter how wild they may be. One parent is sometimes amazed by the revelations of the other, and often each one does not fully appreciate until this time that the other had some of the same thoughts but was afraid to mention them.

14. *Keeping the family together.* One of the major goals of postpartum discussions is to keep the family together both during this early period and in subsequent years. This is best done by working hard to bring out the issues early and by encouraging the parents to talk about their difficult thoughts and feelings as they arise. It is best for them to share their problems with each other. Some couples who do not seem to be close previously may move closer together as they work through the process of adaptation. As with any painful experience, the parents may be much stronger after they have gone through these reactions together.

15. *Adaptation to stress.* Each parent's adaptation depends on his or her background and experience. For many young people this is the most difficult problem that they have ever had to deal with in their lives. However, their past behavior and family experiences often give us a clue as to how they will react and what their individual process of adaptation will be. Some parents have had turbulent earlier periods in their lives with their own mother and father. Under stress they may return to the behavior and responses of that period. In others, if the malformation resembles a malformation in a relative or in himself or herself, one parent may believe he or she is the cause of the malformation and feel tremendously guilty. In most cases this can be discussed and clarified. It may be helpful for parents to explore how they have reacted under stress in the past.

9

BONDING: THE ROUTE

TO INDEPENDENCE

In our practices, many parents voiced two concerns as they approach parenthood: On one hand, they ask, "Will I be able to parent as well as my parents did?" On the other hand, they state, "I don't want to care for my child the way I was cared for." As we learn more about how parents develop a tie to their infant and how the infant develops an attachment to his parents, it appears that this belief that parenting patterns are passed along may be well founded. A multitude of studies have revealed that how we are cared for and nurtured as infants and children affects how we parent, as well as how we interact with all other people. This work has widened our appreciation of the generational effects from parent to child to adult. It appears that the internal working models of parenting are often passed down and become the script the child uses when he or she becomes an adult.

At the same time, there are many opportunities for growth and renewal. As caregivers, we hope to make families aware of these possibilities. The perinatal period—pregnancy, birth, and the postpartum period—is a sensitive time, especially because of the "openness" in this period when advice, support, and new understandings and awarenesses can shape significant changes. There is a possibility for healing, repairing, or changing hurts of the past— for reorganizing in an internal way, for reshaping and creating psychological and behavioral change in the parents and then, in turn, in their child.

The meaning of attachment and bonding in our lives has been dramatized recently by the spate of recent stories circulated by U.S. newspapers about individual traumas of adopted or foster children being reclaimed by their birth parents after a long separation. Newspapers have shown pictures such as ones of a two-year-old called "Jessica" as she reached for her adoptive mother while being taken away from the adoptive parents with whom she had lived for two years, to be returned to her biological parents. Anyone seeing this picture could not help but be moved and saddened by the enormous pain this child experienced as she was being wrenched away from her known and beloved adoptive parents.

Within a few days after one particular photograph of Jessica had appeared, several parents talked to us about the great distress this caused for them. A major reason for their response was the memory of the childhood experiences that this rekindled. For instance, one woman found herself weeping and weeping throughout the day after seeing that picture. In searching for the source of her reactions, she recognized the feelings of abandonment she experienced at a similar age when her mother often left her crying in her crib, telling her she had to learn to be by herself and not cry. In this particular situation the mother wanted the house kept quiet because she was caring for a sick relative. The child experienced this as rejection, loss, and abandonment. Having a two-year-old child of her own now, this woman identified the feelings she would have if her own daughter were taken away. She found herself checking her daughter's room over and over to be sure she was all right.

Another couple, in their distress over the newspaper picture, found themselves overreacting to the politics of the situation, being angry at the judge's decision, and snapping at each other. When they began to discuss why they were so angry, they both recognized that with a daughter about the same age, they were imagining how terrible it would be for her to be taken from them. In their unconscious identification of their own daughter with Jessica, they were displacing their distress onto each other. They also remembered abandonment feelings with mothers and fathers who were not emotionally available to them.

In these situations the early life experiences of these people, who did not feel securely attached and emotionally safe in their families of origin, prompted them to overidentify with the same anxieties and unconsciously project them onto their own children. Parents sometimes re-create, reenact, or try to repair their own unresolved childhood losses through their own child. This can create an overinvolvement or overconcern about their child. In reading about cases such as the removal of adopted children, they are projecting their own experience as a child (fear of loss or separation) onto their own child. For this reason, the picture of another child's sorrow can retrigger enormous feelings of pain and loss. However, another couple might react to Jessica's sadness with great empathy and feeling for her tragic situation, but without identifying with some experience in their own lives. They might recognize how much they had felt loved and secure in their own early childhood, and how much they wished that for Jessica.

What does this tell us about attachment and bonding? Certainly, the potential reverberation throughout one's life of both positive and negative early life experiences is becoming more and more appreciated. In our current knowledge of child development, we recognize that children are deeply affected by loss and need help to adjust. Jessica's situation showed widespread recognition of this problem. The public could empathize with her adoptive parents as they fought in the courts to the bitter end to keep her because they were tightly bonded to her.

The security created by such bonds and the protection and nurturing that follow are the themes we have followed in earlier chapters. Such security, or the lack of it, has reverberations far into our later lives. Part of what gives us our humanity is our ability to feel, to be motivated by emotion, and to have a memory, both conscious and unconscious, of significant past events. Early experiences can resurface unexpectedly and cause untoward reactions without our being able to recognize their source. Jessica's separation from her "psychological parents" touched something deep in everyone who followed her situation, but essentially in those people whose own experience resonates in some way.

The term *bonding,* as we have seen, refers to the parents' emotional investment in their child. It is a process that builds and grows with repeated meaningful and pleasurable experiences. At the same time, another tie, usually referred to as *attachment,* is developing in infants, toward their parents and others who help in their care. It is from this emotional connection that infants can begin to develop a sense of who they are and from which a child can evolve and be able to venture into the world. Without a secure base established in infancy, humans from childhood throughout adult life may develop and cling to the belief that the world is unstable, and that they cannot safely trust others. When a parent feels this emotional connection or bond to the infant, it is much more than just an interest in feeding or changing or tending the infant. It is caring—feeling oneself into the infant's place, sensing and responding to the infant's needs, whether physical or emotional. The infant is powerfully influenced by this emotional investment.

BONDING AND ATTACHMENT

The relationship between concepts of bonding and attachment has a long history.[1] The story started a half century ago with the work mentioned earlier of René Spitz.[2] He noted that babies who were well fed, clothed, and kept warm in an orphanage, but given no emotional attention, holding, or affection, had a syndrome he called "hospitalism." The babies' physical growth and mental development slowed or ceased, and their appetite and weight gain decreased. After a short period of time they lost any interest in interacting, and often they died.

John Bowlby was the first observer to recognize that childhood experiences, and not just inner psychic forces, affect how an individual responds, develops, and acts in his or her own parenting.[3] He further described this process in terms of his model of attachment. "The child builds up an internal representational model of himself," dependent on how he was cared for. In later life this internalized model allows children to be capable of helping themselves and to feel worthy of being helped, should difficulty arise. In the early years of life, this belief in themselves and this sense of security with caregivers not only allows children to separate from their parents when going to nursery school or kindergarten, but also enables them to become independent and explore freely. Thus, each of us has an inner "blueprint" that is in part drawn from how we were parented in our earliest years.

A brilliant discovery essential to our understanding of the attachment process was made by Mary Ainsworth.[4] She first observed and recorded how mothers over the first months of life at home (both in Baltimore and Uganda) responded to their infants' many signals, including crying, smiling, feeding, and eye contact. To determine the quality of attachment of these children to their mothers, she developed the Ainsworth Strange Situation, which is now a well-known research tool.[5] In a setting away from the home, she observed each child in a room full of toys during a series of separations and reunions with the mother. In one period of separation from the mother, a stranger was in the room, while in another period the baby was alone.

The responses and behavior of the one-year-olds were observed while he was in the room with his mother and again during the periods of separation and reunion. Ainsworth discovered that children's responses to the strange situation could be grouped into three general categories and, most significantly, that the infants' responses were related to the styles of parent caregiving that she had previously observed in their homes. In one group of one-year-olds, each child came into the room and, within a short time, began to explore the toys. When the mother left, the child cried for a short time, and when she returned, the child came to her with arms outstretched and then returned to the toys. Ainsworth called this group, which included 60 percent to 65 percent of the children, the "securely attached." Twenty percent to twenty-five percent were termed "avoidant"; while they seemed indifferent to their mothers' presence, even snubbing them on reunion, they cried and showed much more separation distress when their mothers left than did the secure babies. During the home observation, these infants had mothers whom the observers had rated as rejecting, neglectful, or interfering. The 10 percent who were labeled as "ambivalent" children were afraid to explore the room and became anxious and upset on separation, usually crying continuously. On the mothers' return, they sought contact with their mothers but, at the same time, often arched their backs away.

When the mother was responsive, attentive, and sensitive to the unique needs of her baby during its first year, the infant at thirteen months was usually observed in the test situation to have a secure attachment. Although some of the differences in these securely attached children can be related to their personality or inborn characteristics or other factors, their behavior was strongly correlated to the type of parenting the children had received as

young infants. It is of interest that these same qualities of responsiveness and attentiveness are shown by mothers who have early
contact with their infants shortly after birth.

A special note should be made that two studies of premature
and sick infants and one study of healthy full-term infants separated at birth revealed that at thirteen months the normal incidence of secure attachment behaviors was observed. In one study,
twenty-four infants, despite a prolonged separation just after birth
because of prematurity or serious illness, showed patterns of
attachment (secure, insecure, etc.) similar to those of infants who
had not been separated at birth.[6] A similar unpublished observation was made in another group of thirty-one premature infants
studied at eleven months of age. Likewise, thirty healthy full-term
infants who did not receive early or extended time with their
mothers in the first days of life had normal attachment behaviors at
thirteen months.[7] Because women who had a doula during labor
have been shown to feel more relaxed, to feel close to their newborns more quickly, and to view their infants more optimistically
when compared to mothers who did not have support during labor,
it will be important to study such infants' attachment behaviors at
thirteen months. Overall, more research is needed before we can
make a firm link between the extent of early mother–infant contact and the quality of the infant's attachment behaviors, as measured at thirteen months.

Psychologist Alan Stroufe, who has confirmed, continued,
and extended the work of Ainsworth, demonstrated that the
securely based child at thirteen months was securely attached at six
years and that avoidant children at thirteen months were avoidant
at six years.[8] The evidence at present indicates that many children
identified as either securely attached, avoidant, or ambivalent at
thirteen months continue these patterns into adulthood, but there
are, of course, significant exceptions due to later positive and negative events impinging on the children and their parents. As
Stroufe has noted, there are two behavioral characteristics of a

secure attachment relationship in the first two years of life: (1) the ability of the child to find and be reassured by well-known caregivers and (2) the willingness of the child to explore and master the environment when supported by the presence of a caregiver.[9]

However, a secure attachment can be shattered by events that may seem insignificant to adults. In one case from our practice, a baby whom we shall call Charlie was a healthy firstborn with an appealing smile. He showed warm responsiveness with his mother at his well-baby visits. At his fifteen-month visit, he cried when he received his immunizations, but after a smile and a hug from his mother, he settled down and played with the toy his mother had brought for him. After the visit, the nurse commented that Charlie was one of her favorites and added, "He certainly has a secure attachment with his mother."

When the mother next contacted the office two months later, she sounded distressed and angry. "Charlie has been terrible. He won't go to sleep, he's spoiled, and he hangs onto me all day. He won't eat like he did, and he cries and kicks when I try to help him." When questioned about what had happened, she told about the wonderful two-week vacation she and her husband had had in Florida. Charlie had stayed at home with a caregiver recommended by a neighbor. The caregiver said he had cried on and off for two days and nights, but was quiet and cooperative the rest of the time. The mother complained that Charlie "did not know her" when she returned from the vacation. All this was attributed to some inexplicable attitude in the child, not to the effects of separation. With pediatric help, the sleep and eating problems gradually improved over several weeks, but the mother reported many continuing behavior problems and talked about Charlie as a difficult, angry "problem child" for the next six months. The family then left the city, but returned for a visit with the pediatrician and nurses two years later to show off their new child, twenty-month-old Brian. The mother told how she had gradually introduced Brian to a sitter starting at fifteen months and had exposed him to slowly increasing periods of separation over the course of a month before she and her husband had taken a three-day weekend trip. "And Brian hasn't changed from his cooperative behavior since we got back," she said.

Charlie's reaction to the separation is a common one, and the cause is often not appreciated by the parents. The change appears to have been due to Charlie's deep fear of abandonment when his parents were away and his loss of trust in his mother. Other factors may be involved, of course. Charlie and Brian are different genetically and temperamentally. Brian was not alone during the shorter separation from his parents. He had his brother with him, as well as a familiar sitter. Had Charlie's mother not been so devoted and bonded, his distress might have continued and been more severe.

AVOIDING EXCESSIVE SEPARATION STRESS

Separation reactions are almost universal, no matter how close or how distant the parent–child relationship might be, no matter what the type or length of the separation, and no matter whether it was the first or the fiftieth separation. Such reactions are common, complex, and variable. Bowlby suggested that any separation from the mother is important to the child. He considered separation from the mother—the fear of abandonment—to be the primary fear of human beings.

But separations from mothers can educate children if the children are allowed to feel a moderate amount of anxiety, not the unrelieved tension that causes panic. Children can learn self-sufficiency as they find new ways to comfort and to occupy themselves. They discover that other people to whom they are entrusted by a reliable mother can provide care and companionship.

A general pattern of responses to separation exists. In the first five months of life there is usually no clearcut evidence of reaction to a parent's departure; but in the second half of the first year, babies show stranger anxiety and definite reactions to separation. Separation anxiety becomes unmistakable—in some children, by nine months—in the form of whimpering, clinging, prolonged crying, or the intensified use of a comforting object. The sense of loss may become acute considerably earlier than nine months if the separation is extended, as in Spitz's orphanage. The patterned responses, which usually remain the same for each child, rise in a crescendo of intensity and frequency up to eighteen months, or sometimes beyond. The reactions appear earliest in the first year with children who experience significant separations from their mothers, but they are evident in almost all children by the age of one year.

Stranger anxiety—a reaction in which the infant becomes quiet, clouds over, or cries agitatedly at the approach of an unfamiliar person or even at the sound of a new voice—is seen as early as six months and is usual by a year. After the age of one and a half years, most children appear to be less overwhelmed by separation, but they continue to react vigorously to it up to two and a half years. After the age of eighteen months, however, the protests seem to be merged increasingly with annoyance and with the wish to control the mother. Most two-year-olds protest strongly even when the mother's attention is diverted while she talks on the telephone or to another person. By the end of the third year, most children are able to accept separations under ordinary circumstances.

Bowlby suggested that there are great individual differences in young children's ability to tolerate separations.[10] Parents and pediatricians cannot always identify the especially vulnerable children, but we can offer some precautionary suggestions. Differences in mothers, fathers, babies, and family circumstances will lead the wise pediatrician to modify these proposals. The parent can help the child master separation fears. Teaching an infant to wave "bye-bye" is one of the first steps, and an important one, because it gives the child a feeling of participation and mastery. "Peek-a-boo" is another game that reassures a child because he can make his mother appear and disappear at will. Gradually he learns that he can rely on his mother to return, even when she leaves the room or goes out the door with her hat on.

The lack of verbal communication, particularly in the first eighteen months, makes preparation for an absence of more than two days almost impossible. The protests of the baby to separation may seem much more dramatic from one and a half to two and a half years; but observations of children suggest that separation has a more disintegrative effect on the child under eighteen months, who is apt to react with severe anxiety or quiet despair. The trauma of longer separations will be reduced, of course, to the degree that there is a familiar relative to stay with the child. On the other hand, separations for a morning or afternoon will prepare a child for longer absences later on.

THE PROBLEM OF VACATIONS

Young parents are often exposed to a lot of persuasion from relatives, friends, and sometimes doctors to get away from a young child for "a real vacation." The principle of the importance of relief is sound, but an understanding of the vulnerability of the child should help parents to substitute small, tolerable absences for the customary one- or two-week vacation. When unduly long separations cannot be eliminated, the impact can be softened when children remain in their own homes.

Often parents are hurt by the child who ignores them after a separation and are tempted to retaliate in kind or to show anger. These reactions intensify the child's fear of loss. Parents are usually relieved to hear how common and natural is this reaction of ignoring the parents after a separation. Another frequent response in children is an outburst of anger. A parent is almost certain to think—and to be told—that the child is spoiled. The parents may feel the impulse to meet such challenges by tightening up their discipline. In most cases this would be a mistake, because doing so would intensify the child's sense of loss. On the other hand, if parents feel guilty about their absence and allow the child to be abusive or controlling, a new and chronic problem may be created. A middle-of-the-road course, with daily routines back to normal, is best.

Until the last one or two decades, many child psychiatrists and psychologists strongly advocated that children stay home with a consistent caregiver before gradual introduction into nursery school at three years. In spite of this, a few children were not ready to make this separation from their parents until a bit later. With major changes in the roles and responsibilities of women in the last thirty years, most infants have participated in a nationwide uncontrolled experiment in much earlier and more frequent separations. It will be many years before the results are known. Surprisingly, infants appear to have tolerated separations from parents and home at earlier and earlier ages. However, most of the scientific studies have focused on children in high-quality day care and preschools, and it is not clear how this translates to the experiences available to the vast majority of infants and preschoolers. Experts still vigorously debate the question of how well children tolerate these separation experiences in the first year. For those infants who have caregivers at home, the advantages of a relationship for the first two or three years with a consistent, loving, attentive caregiver have been shown repeatedly. However, little is known about the disturbing and disruptive effect on the infant when this caregiver leaves during the first two or three years. And the loss of the consistent caregiver is more the rule than the exception. The effects on the infant are often the same as those encountered when the mother who has been at home is away for several days—angry hitting of the mother and resistance to her loving advances, abject despair, prolonged crying, fussing, irritability, and somatic symptoms such as loss of appetite, weight loss, sleep disturbance, and toilet-training regression. Infants have no sense of time as adults do; an hour or a day is an eternity for them. Before language is well developed and abstract concepts like time are appreciated, verbal preparation and explanation are only partly understood, at best.

What have we learned about helping children with separation during the very sensitive first three years, and particularly the first one and a half to two years, when there is limited language comprehension?

1. Care by one or two consistent, loving caregivers, including or in addition to the parents, is extremely important. There is a Russian saying that you cannot pay anyone enough to do for a child what a mother (parent) does naturally for free. If the parents both work or attend school, can one or both be away from home less than full-time during the three- to five-year preschool period? There is no perfect formula for the ideal loving, consistent caregiver who can be counted on to stay with the infant for three to five years. However, the lives of older women who become caregivers are often more stable than those of most young women. Child care is subject to the same economic pressures as other supply-and-demand services, and an excellent caregiver can be lured away by a family offering more money and better accommodations. Another caregiver such as a grandparent or a neighbor whom the infant knows well can help the infant through the crisis of the loss of a consistent caregiver if one of the parents cannot arrange considerable extra time with the child. The goal for the parent should be to provide loving, consistent care as much as possible. It is also vital to be ready to be very sensitive, thoughtful, compassionate, and tolerant of the infant's behavior for days and weeks if that caregiver leaves.

2. There have appeared to be some advantages to the varied experiences provided for infants due to the separation associated with the parents' work, school, and other out-of-home activities. Most children have shown an ability at early ages to attach to caregivers other than their parents—if the teachers, baby-sitters, or nannies are loving and attentive and are introduced gradually into the children's lives, as a grandparent or neighbor might be. The gradual introduction, with parental support for the infant during many contact hours for two or three weeks before an anticipated parental absence, can greatly reduce the infant's distress. Even with this slow preparation, it is best for parents to be prepared to talk with their one-and-a-half- to two-year-old child (or older) by telephone during their absence if the child appears greatly distressed. And, of course, parents should make sure that the child still has any favorite stuffed animals or other transitional objects. (When children up to one and a half years are distressed by a separation, they may whimper, cry for prolonged periods, or become withdrawn and quiet.)

3. In the first two years, children usually have one or two individuals with whom they have their primary attachment. Even though toddlers relate well and seem attached to three or four adults, when they are tired or frightened it becomes clear that one person, often the mother, is the one with whom they have the principal attachment.

When the parents had early life experiences that may affect their child rearing, certain new methods can help them change their "blueprints." For example, during pregnancy, a brief opportunity to discuss with a therapist some of the grief from the loss of a parent at an early age can help an expectant parent get a fresh start. This may help a parent-to-be avoid feeling distant from his or her baby and help the parent look forward to the coming baby without fear. Debra, described in Chapter 1, was able to redraw some of the lines on her personal blueprint. Once she understood how early life experiences were affecting her perception, she was able to free her unborn baby from her own early experiences. After these sessions she began to care for herself and developed warm feelings for the coming infant.

In another case, a mother had a strong bond with her son, and the child appeared to be securely attached and had begun working through the transition of day care without too much difficulty. But the parents, having come for a consultation, were concerned about their two-year-old's distress. The problem occurred when he was dropped off at day care, and was not able to disengage easily from his father. It was noted that his behavior occurred only with his father, not with his mother. In exploring the father's feelings, he remembered his own childhood experience of his father's leaving the family at a very young age and was projecting some insecurity and feelings of separation onto his son. When he realized that he was giving a hidden message to the boy about not being safe, the father was able to stop this confusing message and feel more comfortable with the safety and security of his son in this new place, and the child was able to adjust easily.

In the cases just cited, a time of vulnerability and openness had arisen in the parental system, but appropriate help and support had made a difference and had created significant internalized change for these mothers, fathers, and their infants. Thus, many blueprints of how children feel about themselves and of how they feel secure in the world can be laid down or affected by how they are treated in the early years. A caregiver of an infant must be able to respond with sensitive awareness on a consistent basis. At the same time, a baby's temperament can shape a parent's responses. For example, many parents will note that a particular child is quiet or fussy or highly active, and then modify their own behavior accordingly. But sometimes a fussy baby becomes exasperating for already overtired parents, and, although they want to be able to, they may not know how to help that particular baby. Some parents recognize their own anger and frustration with such an infant—and realize they may not be acting appropriately. Others may unknowingly project some negative attributes onto the baby, based on their own past experiences or beliefs. In any of these situations parents need some guidance, counseling, or other help to work out the difficulties.

A large study by psychologist Dymphna van den Boom in Holland bears examining.[11] Van den Boom took 100 babies (who had all been described as "fussy" from birth, using the Brazelton scale) and divided them into two groups of 50 each. These children showed other risk factors for potential problems besides "difficult" temperament. They were born into poor, uneducated families with many social and economic pressures. During the first year, the investigators provided three counseling visits of two hours each to one group of mothers in their homes when the babies were between six and nine months of age, while the other group of mothers had no counseling. The intervention strategy was directed at promoting a secure attachment by improving each mother's ability to perceive her infant's signals, accurately monitor the signals, select the appropriate response, and then implement the response. Both groups of fussy children were examined via the Ainsworth Strange Situation test at thirteen months. The group of children whose mothers had received counseling on how to help understand their fussy children better showed 68 percent secure attachment, while the no-treatment group showed 28 percent. Of course this important study must be repeated.

Another intervention that appears promising has been reported by pediatrician Elizabeth Anisfeld.[12] This researcher observed that in a poor, stressed urban population where most of the mothers put young infants in firm plastic infant seats throughout the first year, there was a low incidence of secure attachment behavior at one year. In nonindustrialized societies where most babies were carried on the mother's body through the day and slept with the mother at night, there was almost no infant crying. Drawing on these observations and the idea that increased physical contact would promote greater maternal responsiveness, Anisfeld and her associates carried out a study in which one group of babies was carried on the mother's body in a soft baby carrier (Snugli) that gave more physical contact, and this group was compared to another group that used firm infant seats providing less contact.

When the infants were three months old, the mothers using the soft baby carriers were more responsive to their babies' cries and other cues. When all the infants reached thirteen months, the Ainsworth Strange Situation test was applied, with astounding results. Eighty-three percent of the babies carried on their mother's body in the soft carrier were securely attached, in contrast to 39 percent of the infants from the group that used the firm infant seats. Research with lower-risk populations is needed to find out whether the same effect will be found. These studies illustrate our wonderful power and ability to change, grow, and demonstrate that we are not ordained to follow a certain course forever.

INDEPENDENCE

The number of parents who say they do not want a spoiled child, who are ashamed when their child cries and whines and clings in public, and who resort to spanking "to cure the child" of this behavior makes it clear how much "independence" in a child is valued. Ainsworth's and Stroufe's studies cited earlier demonstrate that the attentive, loving responsiveness of parents and caregivers in the first weeks and months of an infant's life usually results in a securely attached child at one year. The securely attached child feels confident about the parents' love, knows the parents can be trusted to understand and meet his or her needs, and sees the world as a safe place. With this confidence, the securely attached child can be more easily consoled with hugs, or contact with a parent's reassuring face or words, when there is a frightening episode or a minor injury. From dependence in the early months comes later independence. Parental efforts to produce independence too early often result in dependence and fears that may last for a lifetime.

Parents are sometimes surprised at how finely tuned their baby is to their own emotional state. Edward Tronick, T. Berry Brazelton, and others, in a laboratory study discussed earlier, looked at what happened when a mother was asked to maintain an unchanging, neutral expression and was told to be unresponsive to her three-month-old baby's signals.[13] Initially, the baby tried intently to elicit the mother's attention to respond, but after one or two minutes the baby began to fuss and then cry, and then became irritable and finally slumped in the infant seat. Thus, a delicate emotional interplay between parent and infant starts soon after birth and is clearly visible by several months. Babies can quickly get over a brief frustration. However, if a mother is sad for several days, her baby will begin to become distressed and irritable. Babies show their feelings in somewhat different ways than adults do. They refuse feedings and become fussy, and their sleep patterns often change.

Aiding the interchange between mother and infant is an infant's ability, even in the early days of life, to identify the mother by smell, voice, and touch, and by the visual appearance of the mother's face. The close attachment that the infant develops comes about in part from the mother's responsiveness to the infant's signals, which include lip smacking, looking, small baby vocalizations, body movements, eye rubbing, and facial expressions, as noted earlier. Each of these signals is activated by changing internal states and a need to feel comforted, and each mother responds to the individual characteristics and temperament of her infant.

This pattern can sometimes be seen more clearly when it is somehow derailed. As an example, we saw at four and a half months a baby who came to the hospital because of her parents' concern about her lack of responsiveness, delayed development, and slow weight gain. She was noted to have strabismus (crossed eyes). The parents and their physician were concerned that these problems might be related to mental retardation and that her strabismus might be secondary to a brain abnormality. As we observed the mother and baby together, we repeatedly noted that they never made eye contact. When questioned about this, the mother said, "I don't know which eye she is using, so I have stopped trying to look eye-to-eye at her." A brief trial of covering the deviant eye resulted in the mother looking at the uncovered eye more and more of the time. Surgery was then performed on the deviating eye. After surgery, with the baby's eyes both moving together normally, a remarkable change in the interaction of mother and baby occurred, and with this came a surge in development in the next month, with much more smiling and responsiveness. At one year, this baby was following normal growth curves, was on schedule with her development, said three words, and had a warm relationship with her mother.

As we saw earlier, parents need to learn about their own baby's particular signals. If they have a baby who startles easily, for example, they need to speak quietly, hold the baby gently, and not have expectations of immediate responsiveness. This gives the baby more time and quiets the environment. When the individual temperament and needs of the infant are responded to appropriately in this way, a baby will often become much more communicative.

How we parent our children unmistakably affects how they feel about themselves and how they are able to adjust to the life we expect of and for them. But our parenting styles, in turn, are affected by several other conditions, including feelings of being supported by our partners, the support available at labor and birth, and ways that the parent–infant relationship is nurtured in the postpartum period. Added to this are the effects brought about by how we were parented and our past significant experiences, the current sources of stress in our lives, and the values and practices of our culture. All of these factors together affect how we care for our children, how we perceive them, and what conscious or unconscious messages we give them. These changing influences and the openness of new parents create many opportunities to adjust a parent–child relationship. We hope that parents and caregivers can feel encouraged by the new awareness of their potential for supportive parenting.

When parents are consistent in their patterns of care and pay attention to the particular signals of their baby, they provide a highly favorable environment for the child to experience the parents (and the world) as reliable and responsive to its individual needs. The child also needs to feel an emotional connection to the parents in order to respond. Mothers and fathers soon notice that a child's particular kind of cry, desire to be held, clinging behaviors, and efforts to be comforted through being fed or changed are individualized ways of giving signals for attention and affection. When, by trial and error, parents understand what their particular baby needs and make the appropriate response, the infant usually quickly reinforces the parents' efforts by stopping the behavior that originally elicited the parents' attention and becoming quiet, looking eye-to-eye, smiling, or relaxing. By repeated assurance that emotional and physical needs will be met, the baby begins to develop a sense of basic trust.

Notes

INTRODUCTION

1. J. Robertson, *A Baby in the Family: Loving and Being Loved* (London: Penguin Books, 1982).

2. D. W. Winnicott, *The Child, the Family, and the Outside World* (Reading, Mass.: Addison-Wesley/Lawrence, 1987).

3. J. Bowlby, "The Making and Breaking of Affectional Bonds," *British Journal of Psychiatry* 130 (1977): 201–10.

4. R. Spitz, "Hospitalism: An Inquiry into the Genesis of Psychiatric Conditions in Early Childhood," *Psychoanalytic Study of the Child* 1 (1945): 53–75.

5. S. Fraiberg, E. Adelson, and V. Shapiro, "Ghosts in the Nursery: A Psychoanalytic Approach to the Problems of Impaired Infant–Mother Relationships," *Journal of the American Academy of Child Psychiatry* 14 (1975): 387–421.

6. M. D. S. Ainsworth, M. C. Blehar, E. Waters, and S. Wall, *Patterns of Attachment* (Hillsdale, N.J.: Erlbaum, 1978).

7. T. B. Brazelton, *On Becoming a Family* (New York: Delacorte Press/ Lawrence, 1981).

CHAPTER 1: PREGNANCY: NEW CONNECTIONS BEGIN

1. J. M. Steel, F. D. Johnstone, D.A. Hepburn, and A. F. Smith, "Can Pregnancy Care of Diabetic Women Reduce the Risk of Abnormal Babies?" *British Medical Journal* 301 (1990): 1070–74. See also J. Kitzmiller et al., "Preconception Care of Diabetes: Glycemic Control Prevents Congenital Anomalies," *Journal of the American Medical Association* 265 (1991): 731.

2. A. Czeizel and I. Dudás, "Prevention of the First Occurrence of Neural-Tube Defects by Periconceptional Vitamin Supplementation," *New England Journal of Medicine* 327 (1992):1832–35.

3. G. L. Engel, F. Reichman, V. T. Harway, and D. W. Hess, "Monica: Infant-Feeding Behavior of a Mother Gastric Fistula-Fed as an Infant: A Thirty-Year Longitudinal Study of Enduring Effects," in *Parental Influences in Health and Disease,* ed. E. J. Anthony and G. H. Pollack (Boston, Little Brown, 1985), 29–88.

4. T. B. Brazelton, quoted in *Parent–Infant Bonding,* 2nd ed., M. H. Klaus and J. H. Kennell (St. Louis: Mosby, 1982), 12.

5. J. Lumley, "The Image of the Fetus in the First Trimester," *Birth and Family Journal* 7 (1980) 5–14.

6. T. B. Brazelton and B. Cramer, *The Earliest Relationship: Parents, Infants, and the Drama of Early Attachment* (Reading, Mass.: Addison-Wesley/ Lawrence, 1990).

7. T. B. Brazelton, "Effect of Maternal Expectations on

Early Infant Behavior," *Early Child Development of Care* 2 (1973) 259–273.

8. D. B. Cheek, *Hypnosis: The Application of Ideomotor Techniques* (Boston: Allyn & Bacon, 1994).

9. D. W. Winnicott, *The Child, the Family and the Outside World* (Reading, Mass.: Addison Wesley/Lawrence, 1987).

10. T. B. Brazelton, quoted in *Parent–Infant Bonding,* 2nd ed., M. H. Klaus and J. H. Kennell (St. Louis: Mosby, 1982), 16.

11. J. E. Haddow, G. E. Palomaki, G. J. Knight, J. Williams, A. Pulkkinen, J. A. Canick, D. N. Saller, Jr., and G. B. Bowers, "Prenatal Screening for Down's Syndrome with Use of Maternal Screen Markers," *New England Journal of Medicine* 327 (1992): 588–93.

CHAPTER 2: LABOR AND BIRTH

1. P. Simpkin, "Just Another Day in a Woman's Life? Women's Long-Term Perceptions of Their First Birth Experience, Part 1," *Birth* 18 (1991): 203–10. P. Simpkin, "Just Another Day in a Woman's Life? Part 2: Nature and Consistency of Women's Long-Term Memories of Their First Birth Experience," *Birth* 19 (1992): 64–81.

2. D. Korte and R. Scaer, *A Good Birth, a Safe Birth* (Boston: Harvard Common Press, 1992).

3. M. H. Klaus, J. H. Kennell, and P. H. Klaus, *Mothering the Mother* (Reading, Mass.: Addison-Wesley/Lawrence, 1993).

4. W. D. Fraser, S. Marcoux, J. M. Montquin, J. M. Christen, and the Canadian Early Amniotomy Study Group, "Effect of Early Amniotomy on Nulliparous Women," *New England Journal of Medicine* 328 (1993): 1145–49; J. F. R. Barrett, J. Savage, K. Phillips, and R. J. Lilford, "Randomized Trial of Amniotomy in Labor vs. the

Intention to Leave Membranes Intact until the Second Stage," *British Journal of Obstetrics and Gynæcology* 99 (1992): 5–9.

5. I. Chalmers, M. Enkin, and M. J. N. C. Kierse, *Effective Care in Pregnancy* (New York: Oxford University Press, 1989).

6. J. A. Thorp, H. Hu, M. Albin, J. McNutt, B. Meyer, G. R. Cohen, and J. West, "The Effect of Intrapartum Epidural Analgesia on Nulliparous Labor: A Randomized, Controlled Prospective Trial," *American Journal of Obstetrics* 169 (1993): 851–58.

7. L. Fusi, J. A. Maresh, P. J. Steer, and R. W. Beard. "Maternal Pyrexia Associated with the Use of Epidural Analgesia in Labor," *Lancet* 333 (1989): 1250–52.

8. M. C. Klein, R. J. Gauthier, S. H. Jorgensen, J. M. Robbins, J. M. Kaczorowski, B. Johnson et al., "Does Episiotomy Prevent Perineal Trauma and Pelvic Floor Relaxation?" *Journal of Current Clinical Trials* (serial on-line, July 1, 1992), Doc. No. 10; Argentine Episiotomy Trial Collaborative Group, "Routine vs. Selective Episiotomy: A Randomized Controlled Trial," *Lancet* 342 (1993): 1517–18.

9. P. Simpkin, *The Birth Partner* (Boston: Harvard Common Press, 1989).

10. Klaus, Kennell, and Klaus, *Mothering the Mother.*

11. Ibid.

12. W. L. Wolman, "Social Support during Childbirth: Psychological and Physiological Outcomes" (master's thesis, University of Witwatersrand, Johannesburg, 1991).

13. R. Sosa, J. H. Kennell, M. H. Klaus, and S. Robertson, "The Effect of a Supportive Companion on Perinatal Problems, Length of Labor and Mother–Infant Interactions," *New England Journal of Medicine* 303 (1980): 597–600.

14. W. L. Wolman, B. Chalmers, G. J. Hofmeyr, and V. C. Nikodem, "Postpartum Depression and Companionship in the Clinical Birth Environment: A Randomized, Controlled Study," *American Journal of Obstetrics and Gynæcology* 168 (1993): 1388–93.

CHAPTER 3: WHAT THE BABY BRINGS

1. H. F. R. Prechtl and M. J. O'Brien, "Behavioral States of the Full-Term Newborn: The Emergence of a Concept," in *Psychobiology of the Human Newborn,* ed. P. Stratton (New York: Wiley, 1982).

2. P. H. Wolff, *The Development of Behavioral States and the Expression of Emotions in Early Infancy. New Proposal for Investigation* (Chicago, Ill.: Chicago University Press, 1987).

3. R. N. Emde, J. Swedburg, and B. Suzuki, "Human Wakefulness and Biological Rhythms after Birth," *Archives of General Psychiatry* 32 (1975): 780–83.

4. R. L. Fantz, "Visual Experience in Infants: Decreased Attention to Familiar Relative to Novel Ones," *Science* 146 (1964): 668–70.

5. M. M. Haith, T. Bergman, and M. J. Moore, "Eye Contact and Face Scanning in Early Infancy," *Science* 198 (1977): 853–55.

6. J. C. Birnholz and B. R. Benacerraf, "The Development of Human Fetal Hearing," *Science* 222 (1983): 516–18; P. G. Hepper and B. S. Shahidullah, "Development of Fetal Hearing," *Archives of Diseases of Childhood* 71 (1994): F81–F87.

7. A. J. DeCasper and W. P. Fifer, "Of Human Bonding: Newborns Prefer Their Mothers' Voices," *Science* 208 (1980): 1174–76; A. J. DeCasper and P. A. Prescott, "Human Newborns' Perception of Male Voices: Preference, Discrimination, and Reinforcing Value," *Developmental Psychobiology* 17, no. 5 (1984): 481–91.

8. E. M. Blass, V. A. Ciaramitaro, *A New Look at Some Old Mechanisms in Human Newborns: Taste and Tactile Determinants of*

State, Affect, and Action, Monographs of the Society for Research in Child Development, no. 59, serial no. 239 (1994).

9. A. Macfarlane, "Olfaction in the Development of Social Preferences in the Human Neonate." In *Parent—Infant Interaction,* Ciba Foundation Symposium 33 (New York: Associated Scientific Publishers, 1975).

10. M. H. Klaus and P. H. Klaus, *The Amazing Newborn* (Reading, Mass.: Addison-Wesley/Lawrence, 1985).

CHAPTER 4: BIRTH OF A FAMILY: THE FIRST MINUTES AND HOURS

1. K. Christensson, T. Cabrera, E. Christensson, K. Uvnäs-Moberg, and J. Winberg, "Separation Distress Call in the Human Neonate in the Absence of Maternal Body Contact," in *Care of the Newborn Infant: Satisfying the Need for Comfort and Energy Conservation: Thesis of Kyllike Christensson* (Stockholm, Karolinska Institute, 1994).

2. J. A. MacFarlane, D. M. Smith, and D. H. Garrow, "The Relationship between Mother and Neonate," in *The Place of Birth,* ed. S. Kitzinger and J. A. Davis (New York: Oxford University Press, 1978); J. M. Pascoe and J. French, "Development of positive feelings in primiparous mothers toward their normal newborns," *Clinical Pediatrics* 28 (1989): 452–456.

3. K. Robson and R. Kumar, "Delayed Onset of Maternal Affection after Childbirth," *British Journal of Psychiatry* 8 (1967) 13–25.

4. A. M. Widström, A. B. Ransjö-Arvidson, K. Christensson, A. S. Matthiesen, J. Winberg, and K. Uvnäs-Moberg, "Gastric Suction in Healthy Newborn Infants: Effects on Circulation and Developing Feeding Behavior," *ACTA Paediatrica Scandinavica* 76 (1987): 566–72.

5. R. H. Vallardi, J. Porter, and J. Winberg, "Does the Newborn Find the Nipple by Smell?" *Lancet* 344 (1994): 989–90.

6. L. Righard and M. O. Blade, "Effect of Delivery Routines on Success of First Breast-feed," *Lancet* 336 (1990): 1105–7.

7. R. Lang, *Birth Book* (Ben Lomond, Calif.: Genesis Press, 1972).

8. A. M. Widström, W. Wahlburg, A. S. Matthiesen, P. Eneroth, K. Uvnäs-Moberg, S. Wernert, and J. Winburg, "Short-term Effects of Early Suckling and Touch of the Nipple on Maternal Behavior," *Early Human Development* 21 (1990): 153–63.

9. K. Christensson, C. Seles, L. Moreno, A. Belaustequi, P. De La Fuente, H. Lagercrantz, and J. Winberg, "Temperature, Metabolic Adaptation and Crying in Healthy Newborns' Care for Skin-to-Skin or in a Cot," *ACTA Paediatrica Scandinavica* 81 (1992): 488–93.

10. R. Rubin, "Maternal Touch," *Nursing Outlook* 11 (1963): 828–31.

11. M. H. Klaus, J. H. Kennell, N. Plumb, and S. Zuehlke, "Human Maternal Behavior at First Contact with Her Young," *Pediatrics* 46 (1970): 187–92.

12. A. Eidelman, R. Hovars, and M. Kaitz, "Comparative Tactile Behavior of Mothers and Fathers with Their Newborn Infants," *Israeli Journal of Medical Science* 30 (1994): 79–82.

13. W. Trevathan, "Maternal Touch at First Contact with the Newborn Infant," *Developmental Psychology* 14 (1981): 549–58.

14. M. Rödholm and K. Larsson, "The Behavior of Human Male Adults at Their First Contact with a Newborn" (thesis, University of Göteborg, Göteborg, Sweden, 1980).

15. D. W. Winnicott, *Babies and Their Mothers* (Reading, Mass.: Addison-Wesley, 1987), 78.

16. A. McBryde, "Compulsory Rooming-in in the Ward and Private Newborn Service at Duke Hospital," *Journal of the American Medical Association* 145 (1951): 625–28.

17. M. Greenberg, I. Rosenberg, and H. Lind, "First Mothers Rooming-in with Their Newborns: Its Impact on the Mother," *American Journal of Orthopsychiatry* 43 (1973): 783–88.

18. B. Buranasin, "The Effects of Rooming-in on the Success of Breast-feeding and the Decline in Abandonment of Children," *Asia-Pacific Journal of Public Health* 5 (1991): 217–20.

19. a. Data on the Philippines from Molly Pessl, personal communication.
b. Data on Costa Rica: L. Mata, P. Sáenz, J. R. Araya, "Promotion of Breastfeeding in Costa Rica: the Puriscal study," ed. D. B. Jelliffe and E. F. Patrice Jelliffe *Programmes to Promote Breastfeeding* (Oxford, England: Oxford University Press, 1988), 55–69.

20. D. W. Winnicott, *The Child, the Family, and the Outside World.* (Reading, Mass.: Addison-Wesley, 1987), 24.

21. M. H. Klaus, R. Jerauld, N. Kreger, W. McAlpine, M. Steffa, and J. H. Kennell, "Maternal Attachment: Importance of the First Postpartum Days," *New England Journal of Medicine* 286 (1972): 460–63.

22. S. O'Connor, P. M. Vietze, K. B. Sherrod, H. M. Sandler, and W. A. Altemeier, "Reduced Incidence of Parenting Inadequacy Following Rooming-in," *Pediatrics* 66 (1980): 176–82.

23. E. Siegel, K. E. Baumann, E. S. Schaefer, M. M. Saunders, and D. D. Ingram, "Hospital and Home Support During Infancy: Impact on Maternal Attachment, Child Abuse and Neglect, and

Health Care Utilization," *Pediatrics* 66 (1980): 183–90.

24. J. Worobey and J. Belsky, "Employing the Brazelton Scale to Influence Mothering: An Experimental Comparison of Three Strategies," *Developmental Psychology* 18 (1982): 736–43.

25. J. C. Gomez Pedro, "The Effects of Extended Contact in the Neonatal Period on the Behavior of a Sample of Portuguese Mothers and Infants," ed. J. K. Nugent, B. M. Lester, T. B. Brazelton, *The Cultural Context of Infancy,* vol. I, Norwood, N. J.: Ablex, 1989.

26. M. Thompson and R. Westreich, "Restriction of Mother–Infant Contact in the Immediate Postnatal Period," in *Effective Care in Pregnancy,* ed. I. Chalmer, M. Enkin and M. J. N. C. Kierse (Oxford, England: Oxford University Press, 1989), 1328.

27. M. W. Yogman. "Development of the Father–Infant Relationship," in *Theory and Research in Behavioral Pediatrics,* vol. 1, ed. H. Fitzgerald et al. (New York: Plenum Press, 1980).

28. M. Greenberg and N. Morris, "Engrossment: The Newborn's Impact Upon the Father," *American Journal of Orthopsychiatry* 44 (1974) 520–31.

29. R. D. Parke, S. Hymel, T. G. Power, and B. R. Tinsley, "The Father's Role in the Family System," *Seminars Perinatology* 3 (1979): 25–34.

30. D. N. Stern, *The Interpersonal World of the Infant* (New York: Basic Books, 1985).

31. J. Lind, personal communication, 1973.

32. M. Rödholm, "Effects of Father–Infant Postpartum Contact on Their Interaction Three Months after Birth," *Early Human Development* 5 (1981): 79–85.

33. T. B. Brazelton, E. Tronick, L. Adamson, H. Als, and S.

Wise, "Early Mother–Infant Reciprocity," in *Parent–Infant Interaction,* Ciba Foundation Symposium 33 (Amsterdam: Elsevier, 1975).

34. P. H. Wolff, "Observation on Newborn Infants," *Psychosomatic Medicine* 21 (1959): 110–18.

35. Klaus et al., "Human Maternal Behavior."

36. R. Lang, *Birth Book* (Ben Lomond, Calif.: Genesis Press, 1972).

37. K. S. Robson, "The Role of Eye-to-Eye Contact in Maternal– Infant Attachment," *Journal of Child Psychology and Psychiatry* 8 (1967): 13–25.

38. S. Fraiberg, "Blind Infants and Their Mothers: An Examination of the Sign System," in *The Effect of the Infant on the Caregiver,* ed. M. Lewis and L. A. Rosenblum (New York: Wiley, 1974).

39. C. Goren, M. Sarty, and P. Wu, "Visual Following and Pattern Discrimination of Facelike Stimuli by Newborn Infants," *Pediatrics* 56 (1975): 544–49.

40. J. Lind, V. Vuorenkoski, and O. Wasz-Hackert, "Effect of Cry Stimulus on the Temperature of the Lactating Breast of Primiparas," in *Psychosomatic Medicine in Obstetrics and Gynæcology,* ed. N. Morris (Basel, Switzerland: S. Karger, 1973), 293–95.

41. L. Seitamo and O. Wasz-Hackert, "Early-Mother Relationship in the Light of Infant Cry Studies," *ACTA Paedopsychiatrica* 47 (1981): 25–222.

42. W. S. Condon and L. W. Sander, "Neonate Movement Is Synchronized with Adult Speech: Interactional Participation and Language Acquisition," *Science* 183 (1974): 99–101.

43. Ibid.

44. L. W. Sander, G. Stechler, P. Burns, and H. Julia, "Early Mother– Infant Interaction and Twenty-Four-Hour Patterns of Activity and Sleep," *Journal of the American Academy of Child Psychiatry* 9 (1970): 103–23.

45. C. S. Carter, L. L. Getz, and M. Cohen-Parsons, "Relationships between Social Organization and Behavioral Endocrinology in a Monogamous Mammal," *Advances in the Study of Behavior* 16 (1986): 109–45.

46. K. Uvnäs-Moberg and J. Winberg, "Role of Sensory Stimulation in Energy Economy of Mother and Infant with Particular Regard to the Gastrointestinal Endocrine System," in *Textbook of Gastroenterology and Nutrition in Infancy,* 2nd ed., ed. E. Lebenthal (New York: Haven Press, 1989).

47. M. Kaitz, A. Good, A. M. Rokem, and A. I. Eidelman, "Mother's Recognition of Their Newborns by Olfactory Cues," *Developmental Psychobiology* 20 (1987): 5878–91.

48. M. Kaitz, P. Lapidot, R. Branner, and A. Eidelman, "Mothers Can Recognize Their Infants by Touch," *Developmental Psychology* 28 (1992): 35–39.

49. A. N. Meltzoff and M. K. Moore, "Initiation of Facial and Manual Gestures by Human Neonates," *Science* 198 (1977): 75–78.

50. D. W. Winnicott, *Playing and Reality* (London: Tavistock, 1971).

CHAPTER 5: INFANT FEEDING AND THE BEGINNING OF INTIMACY

1. L. Righard and M. O. Alade, "Sucking Technique and Its Effect on the Success of Breastfeeding," *Birth* 19 (1992): 185–89.

2. D. W. Winnicott, *Babies and Their Mothers* (Reading, Mass.: Addison-Wesley/Lawrence 1987), 78.

3. A. Lucas, R. Morley, T. J. Cole, G. Lister, and C. Leeson-Payne, "Breast Milk and Subsequent Intelligence Quotient in Children Born Preterm," *Lancet* 339 (1992): 261–64.

4. M. Makrides, K. Simmer, M. Goggin, and R. A. Gibson, "Erythrocyte Docosahexaenoic Acid Correlates with the Visual Response of Healthy Term Infants," *Pediatrics Research* 34 (1993): 425–27.

5. M. Thompson and R. Westreich, "Restriction of Mother–Infant Contact in the Immediate Postnatal Period," in *Effective Care in Pregnancy,* ed. I. Chalmer, M. Enkin, and M. J. N. C. Kierse (Oxford, England: Oxford University Press, 1989), 1328.

6. A. M. Widstrom, V. Wahlberg, A. S. Matthiesen, P. Eneroth, C. Uvnäs, K. Moberg, S. Wernert, and J. Winberg, "Short-term Effects of Early Suckling and Touch of the Nipple on Maternal Behavior," *Early Human Development* 21 (1990): 153–63.

7. M. DeCarvalho, M. Klaus, and R. Merkatz, "Frequency of Breast-feeding and Serum Bilirubin Concentration," *American Journal of Diseases of Children* 136 (1982): 737.

8. M. DeCarvalho, S. Robertson, A. Friedman, and M. Klaus, "Effect of Frequent Breast-feeding on Early Milk Production and Infant Weight Gain," *Pediatrics* 72 (1983): 307–11.

9. Ibid.

10. S. D. K. Feher, L. R. Berger, J. D. Johnson, and J. B. Wilde, "Increasing Breast Milk Production for Premature Infants with Relaxation/Imagery Audiotape," *Pediatrics* 83 (1989): 57–60.

CHAPTER 6: DEVELOPING TIES: THE FIRST DAYS AND WEEKS

1. D. W. Winnicott, *Collected Papers: Through Pediatrics to Psychoanalysis* (New York: Basic Books, 1958).

2. D. W. Winnicott, *The Child, the Family and the Outside World* (1964; reprint, Reading, Mass.: Addison-Wesley, 1987), 198.

3. B. S. Zuckerman and W. R. Beardsley, "Maternal Depression: A Concern for Pediatrics," *Pediatrics* 79 (1987): 110; A. Stein, D. H. Gath, J. Bucher, A. Bond, A. Day, and P. Cooper, "The Relationship between Postnatal Depression and Mother–Child Interaction," *British Journal of Psychiatry* 154 (1989): 818–23; S. Cogill, H. Caplan, H. Alexandra, K. Robson, and R. Kumar, "Impact of Postnatal Depression on Cognitive Development in Young Children," *British Medical Journal* 292 (1986): 1165–67.

4. E. Tronick, H. Als, L. Adamson, S. Wisu, and T. B. Brazelton, "The Infant's Response to Entrapment between Contradictory Messages in Face-to-Face Interaction," *Journal of the American Academy of Child Psychiatry* 17 (1978): 1–13.

5. M. D. Ainsworth, M. C. Blehar, E. Waters, and S. Wall, *Patterns of Attachment: A Psychological Study of the Strange Situation* (Hillsdale, N.J.: Erlham, 1978).

6. R. G. Barr, S. J. McMullan, H. Spiess et al., "Carrying as Colic Therapy: A Randomized Controlled Trial," *Pediatrics* 87 (1991): 623–30.

7. A. F. Korner, H. C. Kraemer, M. E. Haffner, and E. B. Thoman, "Characteristics of Crying and Non-crying Activity of Full-Term Neonates," *Child Development* 45 (1974): 946–58.

CHAPTER 7: PREMATURE BIRTH AND BONDING

1. D. Prugh, "Emotional Problems of the Premature Infant's Parents," *Nursing Outlook* 1 (1953): 461.

2. D. N. Kaplan and E. A. Mason, "Maternal Reactions to Premature Birth Viewed as an Acute Emotional Disorder," *American Journal of Orthopsychiatry* 30 (1960): 539.

3. L. F. Newman, "Parents' Perceptions of Their Low-Birth-Weight Infants," *Paediatrician* 9 (1980): 182.

4. M. Green, "Parent Care in the Intensive Care Unit," *American Journal of Diseases of Children* 133 (1979): 1119.

5. H. Als, G. Lawhon, F. H. Duffy et al., "Individualized Developmental Care for the Very Low-Birth-Weight Preterm Infant," *Journal of the American Medical Association* 272 (1994): 853.

6. A. Korner, H. Kraemer, and M. Haffner, "Effects of Waterbed Flotation on Premature Infants: A Pilot Study," *Pediatrics* 56 (1975): 361; L. Kramer and M. Pierpont, "Rocking Waterbed and Auditory Stimuli to Enhance Growth of Preterm Infants," *Journal of Pediatrics* 88 (1976): 297.

7. F. Scafidi, T. Field, S. Schomberg et al., "Massage Stimulates Growth in Preterm Infants: A Replication," *Infant Behavior and Development* 13 (1990): 167.

8. P. Gorski, "Premature Infant Behavioral and Physiological Responses to Caregiving Interventions in the Intensive Care Nursery," in *Frontiers of Infant Psychiatry,* ed. J. D. Call, E. Galenson, and R. L. Tyson (New York: Basic Books, 1983).

9. Als et al., "Individualized Developmental Care."

10. E. B. Thoman, E. W. Ingersoll, and C. Acebo, "Premature Infants Seek Rhythmic Stimulation, and the Experience Facilitates

Neurobehavioral Development," *Journal of Developmental Behavioral Pediatrics* 12 (1991): 11–18.

11. N. P. Mann, L. Haddow, L. Stokes, S. Goodley, and N. Ruther, "Effect of Night and Day on Preterm Infants in a Newborn Nursery: Randomized Trial," *British Medical Journal* 293 (1986): 1265–67.

12. C. R. Barnett, P. H. Leiderman, R. Grobstein, and M. Klaus, "Neonatal Separation: The Maternal Side of Interactional Deprivation," *Pediatrics* 45 (1970): 197–205.

13. M. H. Klaus, J. H. Kennell, N. Plumb, and S. Zuehlke, "Human Maternal Behavior at First Contact with Her Young," *Pediatrics* 46 (1970): 187–92.

14. A. D. Leifer, P. H. Leiderman, C. R. Barnett, and J. A. Williams, "Effects of Mother–Infant Separation on Maternal Attachment Behavior," *Child Development* 43 (1972): 1203–18.

15. M. H. Klaus and J. H. Kennell, *Parent–Infant Bonding* (St. Louis: Mosby, 1982), 172.

16. R. G. Harper, C. Sia, S. Sokal, and M. Sokal, "Observations on Unrestricted Parental Contact with Infants in the Neonatal Intensive Care Unit," *Journal of Pediatrics* 89 (1976): 441–45.

17. D. H. Garrow, "Special Care without Separation: High Wycombe, England," in *Parent–Baby Attachment in Premature Infants,* ed. J. A. Davis, M. P. M. Richards, and N. R. C. Robertson (New York: St. Martin's, 1983).

18. J. H. Kennell and M. H. Klaus, "The Perinatal Paradigm: Is It Time for a Change?" in *Clinics in Perinatology* (Philadelphia: Saunders, 1984).

19. J. Torres Pereyra, "The Sotero Del Rio Hospital Santiago

Chile," in *Parent–Baby Attachment in Premature Infants,* ed. J. A. Davis, M. P. M. Richards, and N. R. C. Roberton (New York: St. Martin's, 1983).

20. E. Kahn, S. Wayburne, and M. Fouche, "The Baragwanath Premature Baby Unit—An Analysis of the Case Records of 1000 Consecutive Admissions," *South African Medical Journal* 28 (1954): 453–56.

21. N. Tafari, N. and G. Sterky, "Early discharge of low birth-weight infants in a developing country," *Environmental Child Health* 20 (1974), 73–76.

22. A. Levin, "The Mother–Infant Unit at Tallinn Children's Hospital, Estonia: A Truly Baby-Friendly Unit," *Birth* 21 (1994): 39–45.

23. G. C. Anderson, "Current Knowledge about Skin-to-Skin Kangaroo Care for Preterm Infants," *Journal of Perinatology* 11 (1991): 216–26.

24. A. Whitelaw, G. Heisterkamp, K. Sleath, D. Acolet, and M. Richards, "Skin-to-Skin Contact for Very Low-Birth-Weight Infants and Their Mothers: A Randomized Trial of 'Kangaroo Care.'" *Archives of Diseases of Childhood* 63 (1988): 1377–81.

25. K. Minde, B. Shosenberg, P. Marton, J. Thompson, J. Ripley, and S. Burns, "Self-Help Groups in a Premature Nursery—A Controlled Evaluation," *Journal of Pediatrics* 96 (1980): 933–40.

26. K. Barnard, quoted in *Parent–Infant Bonding,* M. Klaus, and J. H. Kennell (St. Louis: Mosby, 1982), 180.

27. K. Minde, S. Trehub, C. Corter, C. Boukydis, L. Celhoffer, and P. Marton, "Mother–Child Relationships in the Premature Nursery: An Observational Study," *Pediatrics* 61 (1978): 373–79.

28. A. Blake, A. Stewart, and D. Turcan, in *Parent–Infant*

Interaction, Ciba Foundation Symposium 33 (Amsterdam: Elsevier, 1975).

29. T. M. Field, "Effects of Early Separation, Interactive Defects," *Child Development* 48 (1977): 736–71.

30. D. W. Winnicott, "The Mirror Role of Mother and Family in Child Development," in *Playing and Reality* (London: Tavistock, 1971).

31. C. Trevarthan, "Descriptive Analyses of Infant Communicative Behaviour," in *Studies in Mother–Infant Interaction,* ed. H. R. Schaffer (New York: Academic Press, 1977).

32. Field, "Effects of Early Separation."

33. D. Spiker, J. Ferguson, and J. Brooks-Gunn, "Enhancing Maternal Interactive Behavior and Child Social Competence in Low-Birth-Weight, Premature Infants," *Child Development* 64 (1993): 754–68; M. E. Barrera, P. L. Rosenbaum, and C. E. Cunningham, "Early Home Intervention with Low-Birth-Weight Infants and Their Parents," *Child Development* 57 (1986): 20–33.

CHAPTER 8: BIRTH DEFECTS AND BONDING

1. B. Bettelheim, "How Do You Help a Child Who Has a Physical Handicap?" *Ladies Home Journal* 89 (1972): 34–35.

2. N. Johns, "Family Reactions to the Birth of a Child with a Congenital Abnormality," *Medical Journal of Australia* 1 (1971): 277–282.

3. E. Roskies, *Abnormality and Normality: The Mothering of Thalidomide Children* (New York: Cornell University Press, 1974).

4. E. D'Arcy, "Congenital Defects: Mothers' Reactions to First Information," *British Medical Journal* 3 (1968): 796–98.

5. D. Drotar, N. Irvin, J. H. Kennell, and M. H. Klaus, "The Adaptation of Parents to the Birth of an Infant with a Congenital Malformation: A Hypothetical Model," *Pediatrics* 56 (1975): 710–17.

6. M. Dorris, *The Broken Cord* (New York: HarperCollins, 1989).

7. J. Shonkoff, P. Hauser-Cram, M. W. Krauss, and C. C. Upshur, *Development of Infants with Disabilities and Their Families: Implications for Theory and Service Delivery,* Monograph of the Society for Research in Child Development, serial no. 230, vol. 57, no. 6, 1992.

8. A. J. Solnit and M. H. Stark, "Mourning and the Birth of a Defective Child," *Psychoanalytic Study of the Child* 16 (1961): 523–37.

9. M. Voysey, "Impression Management by Parents with Disabled Children," *Journal of Health and Social Behavior* 13 (1972): 80–89.

10. M. Pollak, *Textbook of Developmental Paediatrics* (Edinburgh: Churchill Livingston, 1993), 483–91.

11. S. S. Cook, "Impact of the Disabled Child on the Family," in *Dying and Disabled Children,* ed. H. Dick, D. Roye, Jr., P. R. Buschman, A. Katscher, B. Rubinstein, and F. Forstenzer (New York: Harcourt Press, 1988).

12. L. L. Daniels and G. M. Berg, "The Crisis of Birth and Adaptive Patterns of Amputee Children," Clinical Proceedings, Children's Hospital, Washington, D.C. 24 (1968): 108–17.

13. S. Olshansky, "Chronic Sorrow: A Response to Having a Mentally Defective Child," *Social Casework* 73 (1962): 190–93.

14. A. Solnit, quoted in *Parent–Infant Bonding,* ed. M. H.

Klaus and J. H. Kennell (St. Louis: Mosby, 1982).

15. M. Green, quoted in *Parent–Infant Bonding,* ed. M. H. Klaus and J. H. Kennell (St. Louis: Mosby, 1982).

16. J. Lampe, M. A. Trause, J. H. Kennell, "Parental Visiting of Sick Infants: The Effect of Living at Home prior to Hospitalization," *Pediatrics* 59 (1977): 294–96.

CHAPTER 9: BONDING: THE ROUTE TO INDEPENDENCE

1. R. Karen, *Becoming Attached* (New York: Warner Books, 1994). (Contains a detailed and beautifully written account of the studies of attachment.)

2. R. Spitz, "Hospitalization: An Inquiry into the Genesis of Psychiatric Conditions in Early Childhood," *The Psychoanalytic Study of the Child,* vol. 1 (1945), 53–74.

3. J. Bowlby, *A Secure Base: Clinical Applications of Attachment Theory* (London: Routledge, 1988).

4. M. D. S. Ainsworth, *Infancy in Uganda: Infant Care and the Growth of Love* (Baltimore: Johns Hopkins University Press, 1967).

5. M. D. S. Ainsworth, M. C. Blehar, E. Waters, and S. Wall, *Patterns of Attachment: A Psychological Study of the Strange Situation* (Hillsdale, N.J.: Erlbaum, 1978).

6. S. E. Rode, P. Chang, R. O. Fisch, and L. A. Stroufe, "Attachment Patterns of Infants Separated at Birth," *Developmental Psychology* 17 (1981): 188–91.

7. B. Myers, "Mother–Infant Bonding: The Status of the Critical Period Hypothesis," *Developmental Review* 4 (1984): 262–63.

8. L. A. Stroufe, N. E. Fox, V. R. Pancake, "Attachment and Dependency in the Developmental Perspective," *Child Development* 54 (1983): 1615–27.

9. L. A. Stroufe, "Socioemotional Development," in *Handbook of Infant Development,* ed. J. Osofsky (New York: Wiley, 1979).

10. J. Bowlby, "Separation Anxiety: A Critical Review of the Literature," *Journal of Child Psychology and Psychiatry* 1 (1961): 251.

11. D. van den Boom, "The Influence of Temperament and Mothering on Attachment and Exploration: An Experimental Manipulation of Sensitive Responsiveness among Lower-Class Mothers with Irritable Infants," *Child Development* 65 (1994): 1457–77.

12. E. Anisfeld, V. Casper, W. Nozyce, and N. Cunningham, "Does Infant Carrying Promote Attachment? An Experimental Study of the Effects of Increased Physical Contact on the Development of Attachment," *Child Development* 61 (1990): 1617–27.

13. E. Tronick, H. Als, L. Adamson, S. Wise, and T. B. Brazelton, "The Infant's Response to Entrapment between Contradictory Messages in Face-to-Face Interaction," *Journal of Child Psychiatry* 17 (1978): 1–13.

Index

A Full List of Cedar Books

While every effort is made to keep prices low, it is sometimes necessary to increase prices at short notice. Mandarin Paperbacks reserves the right to show new retail prices on covers which may differ from those previously advertised in the text or elsewhere.

The prices shown below were correct at the time of going to press.

All these books are available at your bookshop or newsagent, or can be ordered direct from the address below. Just tick the titles you want and fill in the form below.

Cash Sales Department, PO Box 5, Rushden, Northants NN10 6YX.
Fax: 01933 414047 : Phone: 01933 414000.

Please send cheque, payable to 'Reed Book Services Ltd.', or postal order for purchase price quoted and allow the following for postage and packing:

£1.00 for the first book, 50p for the secohd; **FREE POSTAGE AND PACKING FOR THREE BOOKS OR MORE PER ORDER.**

NAME (Block letters) ....

ADDRESS ....

....

☐ I enclose my remittance for ....

☐ I wish to pay by Access/Visa Card Number ⬚⬚⬚⬚⬚⬚⬚⬚⬚⬚⬚⬚⬚⬚⬚⬚

Expiry Date ⬚⬚⬚⬚

Signature ....

Please quote our reference: MAND